Philippians

The Mind of Christ

JOHN A. STEWART

Lamplighters International is a Christian ministry that helps individuals engage with God and His Word and equips believers to be disciple-makers.

For additional information about Lamplighters ministry resources, contact:

Lamplighters International
771 NE Harding Street, Suite 250
Minneapolis, MN USA 55413
or visit our website at
www.LamplightersUSA.org.

Product Code: Ph-NK-2P

ISBN 978-1-931372-65-7

CONTENTS

How to Use This Study

What Is Lamplighters?

Lamplighters is a Christian ministry that helps individuals engage with God and His Word and equips believers to be disciple-makers. This Bible study, comprising eight individual lessons, is a self-contained unit and an integral part of the entire discipleship ministry. When you have completed the study, you will have a much greater understanding of a portion of God's Word, with many new truths that you can apply to your life.

How to study a Lamplighters Lesson

A Lamplighters study begins with prayer, your Bible, the weekly lesson, and a sincere desire to learn more about God's Word. The questions are presented in a progressive sequence as you work through the study material. You should not use Bible commentaries or other reference books (except a dictionary) until you have completed your weekly lesson and met with your weekly group. Approaching the Bible study in this way allows you to personally encounter many valuable spiritual truths from the Word of God.

To gain the most out of the Bible study, find a quiet place to complete your weekly lesson. Each lesson will take approximately 45–60 minutes to complete. You will likely spend more time on the first few lessons until you are familiar with the format, and our prayer is that each week will bring the discovery of important life principles.

The writing space within the weekly studies provides the opportunity for you to answer questions and respond to what you have learned. Putting answers in your own words, and including Scripture references where appropriate, will help you personalize and commit to memory the truths you have learned. The answers to the questions will be found in the Scripture references at the end of each question or in the passages listed at the beginning of each lesson.

If you are part of a small group, it's a good idea to record the specific dates that you'll be meeting to do the individual lessons. Record the specific dates each time the group will be meeting next to the lesson titles on the Contents page. Additional lines have been provided for you to record when you go through this same study at a later date.

The side margins in the lessons can be used for the spiritual insights you glean from other group or class members. Recording these spiritual truths will likely be a spiritual help to you and others when you go through this study again in the future.

AUDIO INTRODUCTION

A brief audio introduction is available to help you learn about the historical background of the book, gain an understanding of its theme and structure, and be introduced to some of the major truths. Audio introductions are available for all Lamplighters studies and are a great resource for the group leader; they can also be used to introduce the study to your group. To access the audio introductions, go to www.LamplightersUSA.org.

"DO YOU THINK?" QUESTIONS

Each weekly study has a few *"do you think?"* questions designed to help you to make personal applications from the biblical truths you are learning. In the first lesson the *"do you think?"* questions are placed in italic print for easy identification. If you are part of a study group, your insightful answers to these questions could be a great source of spiritual encouragement to others.

PERSONAL QUESTIONS

Occasionally you'll be asked to respond to personal questions. If you are part of a study group you may choose not to share your answers to these questions with the others. However, be sure to answer them for your own benefit because they will help you compare your present level of spiritual maturity to the biblical principles presented in the lesson.

A FINAL WORD

Throughout this study the masculine pronouns are frequently used in the generic sense to avoid awkward sentence construction. When the pronouns *he*, *him*, and *his* are used in reference to the Trinity (God the Father, Jesus Christ, and the Holy Spirit), they always refer to the masculine gender.

This Lamplighters study was written after many hours of careful preparation. It is our prayer that it will help you "… grow in the grace and knowledge of our Lord and Savior Jesus Christ. To Him be the glory both now and forever. Amen" (2 Peter 3:18).

What Is an Intentional Discipleship Bible Study?
The *Next Step* in Bible Study

The Lamplighters Bible study series is ideal for individual, small group, and classroom use. This Bible study is also designed for Intentional Discipleship training. An Intentional Discipleship (ID) Bible study has four key components. Individually they are not unique, but together they form the powerful core of the ID Bible study process.

1. Objective: Lamplighters is a discipleship training ministry that has a dual objective: (1) to help individuals engage with God and His Word and (2) to equip believers to be disciple-makers. The small group format provides extensive opportunity for ministry training, and it's not limited by facilities, finances, or a lack of leadership staffing.

2. Content: The Bible is the focus rather than Christian books. Answers to the study questions are included within the study guides, so the theology is in the study material, not in the leader's mind. This accomplishes two key objectives: (1) It gives the group leader confidence to lead another individual or small group without fear, and (2) it protects the small group from theological error.

3. Process: The ID Bible study process begins with an Open House, which is followed by a 6–14-week study, which is followed by a presentation of the Final Exam (see graphic on page 8). This process provides a natural environment for continuous spiritual growth and leadership development.

4. Leadership Development: As group participants grow in Christ, they naturally invite others to the groups. The leader-trainer (1) identifies and recruits new potential leaders from within the group, (2) helps them register for online discipleship training, and (3) provides in-class leadership mentoring until they are both competent and confident to lead a group according to the ID Bible study process. This leadership development process is scalable, progressive, and comprehensive.

OVERVIEW OF THE LEADERSHIP TRAINING AND DEVELOPMENT PROCESS

There are three stages of leadership training in the Intentional Discipleship process: (1) leading studies, (2) training leaders, and (3) multiplying groups (see appendix for greater detail).

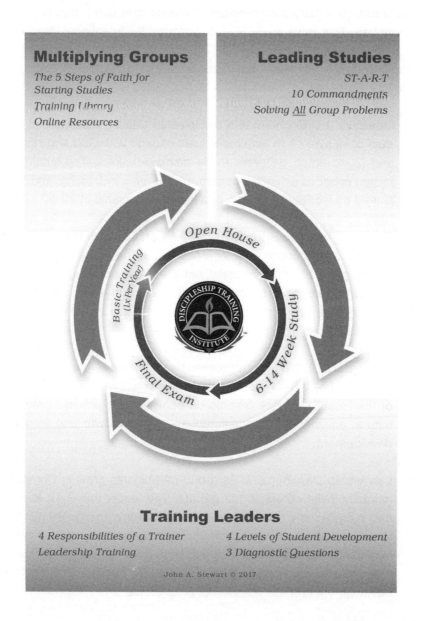

Multiplying Groups

The 5 Steps of Faith for
Starting Studies
Training Library
Online Resources

Leading Studies

ST-A-R-T
10 Commandments
Solving All Group Problems

Open House

Basic Training (1x Per Year)

6-14 Week Study

Final Exam

Training Leaders

4 Responsibilities of a Trainer
Leadership Training

4 Levels of Student Development
3 Diagnostic Questions

John A. Stewart © 2017

How Can I Be Trained?

Included within this Bible study is the student workbook for Level 1 (Basic Training). Level 1 training is both free and optional. Level 1 training teaches you a simple 4-step process (ST-A-R-T) to help you prepare a life-changing Bible study and 10 proven small group leadership principles that will help your group thrive. To register for a Level 1 online training event, either as an individual or as a small group, go to www.LamplightersUSA.org/training or www.discipleUSA. org. If you have additional questions, you can also call 800-507-9516.

ONE

SEEING GOD'S HAND IN CHANGE

Read Philippians 1:1–11; other references as given.

The book of Philippians is often regarded as God's spiritual manual on joy and rejoicing—but it's more than that. Philippians is God's revelation to man, especially believers, on how to think and act in a world whose values and priorities are contrary and often hostile to God and His people.

When we possess the mind of Christ, trials become opportunities to glorify God (chapter 1); service to God and others becomes a joy rather than a burden (chapter 2); personal achievement is exposed as vanity, and life priorities are transformed (chapter 3) and thoughts and actions become personal acts of worship (chapter 4).

In this first lesson, you'll learn how God intervened in Paul's life (and ministry) and redirected his life to greater ministry outreach.

Now ask God to reveal Himself to you through His inspired Word and transform you into the image of Christ.

1. The book of Acts describes the Apostle Paul's three missionary journeys (Acts 13:3–14:26; 15:40–18:22; 18:23–21:17) and the church's expansion into Western civilization. During Paul's second missionary journey, he received a vision at Troas (western Turkey) of a man from Macedonia asking for help (Acts 16:9–10). Some Bible scholars believe the man was Luke (physician and writer of Acts and the gospel of Luke) because of the abrupt change to the plural

Lombardi Time Rule:

If the leader arrives early, he or she has time to pray, prepare the room, and greet others personally.

ADD GROUP INSIGHTS BELOW

pronoun "we" in the verses following the vision. Believing God sent this vision, Paul and his missionary companions sailed across the Aegean Sea to Macedonia, landed at Neapolis, and traveled to Philippi (Acts 16:11–12).

a. Paul's visit to Macedonia was the beginning of Christian missionary expansion to Europe. List three individuals or groups of people whose lives were transformed during Paul's original visit to Philippi (Acts 16:11–34).

_____

_____

_____

b. What did Paul and Silas tell the jailer who asked them, **Sirs, what must I do to be saved?** (Acts 16:30–31)?

_____

_____

2. Philip II, father of Alexander the Great, founded the city of Philippi in 356 BC to control the gold mines in the region. After the Battle of Philippi in 42 BC, the city became a Roman colony, and its people were granted Roman citizenship. As Roman citizens, they received many privileges, including autonomous government and immunity from paying taxes. The Philippians were particularly proud of being Roman citizens (Acts 16:20–21). Although the consistent use of the personal pronoun "I" throughout the book indicates that Paul was the singular writer of the letter, he and Timothy, already known by the church (Philippians 2:20), jointly greeted the Philippians. To what three groups of people is Paul's letter addressed (Philippians 1:1)?

1. _____

2. _____

3. _____

3. Paul addresses his letter to all the Philippian believers (saints), and he extends a special greeting to the bishops (overseers, pastors) and deacons (Philippians 1:1). Many Bible scholars believe the church began in Acts 2, but the first mention of men serving in the office of deacon/servant occurs in Acts 6. Therefore, a church isn't required to have deacons, but if it does, they must be biblically qualified. What are the qualifications of men who serve in this important ministry (1 Timothy 3:8–12)?

    _____

    _____

    _____

    _____

    _____

    _____

    _____

    _____

4. Paul used the word **saint** (Philippians 1:1, Greek *hagios*) to describe believers in Philippi. In general religious language, *saint* describes (1) a deceased individual who has been officially recognized, especially through canonization, as preeminent for holiness; (2) a normal Christian person; (3) an individual of unusual holiness or piety; or (4) a person of a particular religious group such as the Latter-day Saints (Mormons). Which one of these definitions *do you think* Paul meant in verse one (Philippians 1:1; 1 Corinthians 1:2)? Why?

    _____

    _____

    _____

5. Paul began his letter by identifying Timothy and himself as servants (Gk. *doulos*: "slaves, servants") of God (Philippians

Zip-It Rule:

Group members should agree to disagree, but should never be disagreeable.

ADDITIONAL INSIGHTS

1:1). Then he offered the standard early church blessing—grace and peace. In all seventeen occurrences of the phrase **grace and peace** in the New Testament, the word **grace** comes before **peace**. When a believer accepts God's grace (in salvation), he receives peace with God and should be thankful. What two things was Paul particularly thankful for (Philippians 1:5)?

1. _____

   _____

2. _____

   _____

6. a. The book of Philippians was written ten years after Paul evangelized the city. The Philippians remained faithful to God and to the apostle Paul during those ten years (Acts 16:11–12). What spiritual promise did God give the Philippians (and all believers) to help them remain faithful to the Lord (Philippians 1:6)?

   _____

   _____

   _____

   b. Many Christians are afraid they'll fall away from the faith and bring reproach on Jesus' name. Some, then, refuse to live wholeheartedly for Christ. What must every Christian do to ensure he will never fall away from Jesus Christ (2 Peter 1:5–7)?

   _____

   _____

   _____

   _____

   _____

   _____

c. If a believer allows the eight spiritual qualities listed in 2 Peter 1:5–7 to be developed in his life, God promises him four things. What are they (2 Peter 1:8–11)?

1. _____

2. _____

3. _____

4. _____

Want to learn how to disciple another person, lead a life-changing Bible study or start another study? Go to www.Lamplighters USA.org/training to learn how.

ADDITIONAL INSIGHTS

7. The phrase **the day of Jesus Christ** (Philippians 1:7) appears six times in the New Testament, three of those in Philippians (Philippians 1:6, 10; 2:16). The phrase refers to a future time when Christ judges and rewards believers. The more common but distinct phrase **the day of the Lord** refers to a future time of judgment when Christ returns to judge those who are not saved. Some Christians are surprised to learn they will eventually face judgment. What do the following verses teach about the future judgment of the believer?

a. The judge and the place of judgment (1 Corinthians 4:4–5; 2 Corinthians 5:10)

_____

_____

b. The measure or basis of judgment (1 Corinthians 4:3–5)

_____

_____

c. If you faced Jesus Christ in judgment tomorrow, what, if any, things would you change today?

_____

_____

8. Paul mentioned his imprisonment for the first time in Philippians 1:7. He was likely imprisoned in Rome because

he sent greetings from those of Caesar's household (Philippians 4:22). Paul said his ministry included both the defense and confirmation of the gospel (Philippians 1:7). What *do you think* the difference is between Paul's ministry of defending and of confirming the gospel?

_____

_____

_____

_____

9. Paul told the Philippians *how* he prayed for them (Philippians 1:4, **with joy**) and *why* he prayed for them (Philippians 1:7, they were **in his heart**).

    a. What did Paul pray for the Philippians (Philippians 1:9–11)?

        _____

        _____

        _____

    b. What was Paul's ultimate objective for the Philippian believers (Philippians 1:9–11)?

        _____

        _____

        _____

        _____

Two

The Purpose of Life

Read Philippians 1:12–30; other references as given.

Paul expressed his deep love for the Philippians (Philippians 1:1–11). He wanted them to grow spiritually so they would choose **the things that are excellent** and ultimately bring more glory to God.

In this lesson, Paul reassures the Philippians that God has used his circumstances as a prisoner in Rome to advance the gospel. To Paul, proclaiming the gospel was so important that being in prison was a small price to pay for such a great reward.

Now ask God to reveal Himself to you through His inspired Word and transform you into the image of Christ.

1. Paul was a warrior for Jesus Christ—a soldier of the cross. He was scourged five times, beaten with rods three times, stoned, shipwrecked three times, and spent a day and night in the sea (2 Corinthians 11:24–25). He faced threats from thieves, Gentiles, and false brethren (2 Corinthians 11:26). He was often tired from toil yet spent many nights without sleep. He was often hungry, thirsty, and cold (2 Corinthians 11:27). But still he pressed on, ministering to the churches and preaching the gospel of salvation to those without Christ in their lives.

    a. As Paul conducted mission work, he was arrested in Jerusalem and eventually imprisoned in Rome. Rather than resenting God or becoming discouraged, he

Volunteer Rule:

If the leader asks for volunteers to read, pray, and answer the questions, group members will be more inclined to invite newcomers.

ADD GROUP INSIGHTS BELOW

accepted imprisonment as God's sovereign plan for his life. List three positive things that occurred while Paul was imprisoned (Philippians 1:12–14).

_____

_____

_____

b. The apostle's statement, **the things *which happened*** (Philippians 1:12), indicates that his arrest and imprisonment were unanticipated, interrupting his missionary plans. The statement, **have actually turned out,** (Philippians 1:12) shows that Paul was unable to see God's plan until sometime *after* his imprisonment. List at least two important spiritual truths that Philippians 1:12 teaches about how God reveals His will to believers— even His choicest servants.

1. _____

_____

2. _____

_____

2. Paul's imprisonment caused some of the brethren to more boldly witness for Jesus Christ (Philippians 1:14). Some preached the Word with pure intentions. Others, however, were motivated by envy, strife, and selfish ambition, hoping to cause Paul trouble (Philippians 1:15–17). What was Paul's response to the preaching of God's Word by both groups (Philippians 1:18)?

_____

_____

3. a. The Bible instructs Christians to do good works with pure motives (1 Corinthians 10:31–33; Ephesians 4:1–3; Philippians 2:3). In Philippians 1:15–18, however, Paul seems unconcerned whether Christians have pure

motives when they preach to others. If Paul isn't rejoicing in believers serving with impure motives, what is Paul rejoicing in (Philippians 1:18)?

_____

_____

b. In what way(s) *do you think* Paul's statement in Philippians 1:18 emphasizes the importance of preaching the gospel to the lost?

_____

_____

_____

c. If you are a Christian, do you faithfully share your faith in Jesus Christ with the lost, or are you satisfied to just attend church each week?

_____

What could you do to become a more effective witness for Christ and make disciples of all nations?

_____

_____

_____

4. Paul wrote to the Philippians while in prison (Philippians 1:13). Under Roman law, an individual could be held in prison for an extended time while awaiting trial, but not as a punishment. Once a prisoner was tried, he was executed, punished, or released. Paul was optimistic that God would deliver him in response to the Philippians' prayers and by the help of the Holy Spirit (**the Spirit of Jesus Christ**; the Greek can be translated "of" or "from" Jesus Christ; John 16:7).

a. Philippians 1:21 is Paul's spiritual mission statement: **For to me, to live is Christ, and to die is gain.** Although this verse is familiar to many Christians, many don't fully understand its meaning. Using Philippians 1:20–22, develop a more comprehensive definition of Paul's statement, **to live is Christ, and to die is gain**.

_____

_____

_____

_____

b. Some people worship their work, work at their play, and play at their worship. Now that you have a more complete understanding of Paul's personal mission statement (Philippians 1:21), prepare your own one-sentence spiritual mission statement. Begin your statement, _The ultimate goal of my life as a disciple of Jesus Christ is_ _____

_____

_____

5. Paul instructed the Philippians to conduct themselves in a manner **worthy of the gospel of Christ** (Philippians 1:27). The Greek word _politeuomai_ means "to be a citizen, to conduct one's self as a citizen." Likely, to make an important point Paul was comparing the Philippian believers' Roman citizenship to their standing before Christ.

a. Of what country, nation, or kingdom is every Christian a citizen (Philippians 3:20)?_____

_____

Does that include you? _____

_____

If you're uncertain about your eternal destiny, please turn to the back of this Bible study and read the "Final Exam."

b. Only when a believer fully understands his heavenly citizenship can he fully embrace his *present* calling to tell unbelievers about salvation through Jesus Christ. What is a believer's current role and responsibility on earth as a citizen of heaven (2 Corinthians 5:18–20)?

_____

_____

c. Hebrews 11 is often called the "Hall of Faith" because it highlights several Old Testament saints and their heroic acts of faith. How did these spiritual giants of faith regard this world and their eternal home (Hebrews 11:10–16)?

_____

_____

_____

_____

_____

6. In what way(s) do you think a believer's heavenly *citizenship* and his or her *commission* as Christ's ambassador on earth should affect his or her life and service for God?

_____

_____

_____

_____

7. What specific things did Paul instruct the Philippians to do to live worthy of the gospel of Jesus Christ (Philippians 1:27–29)?

_____

_____

_____

35% Rule:

If the leader talks more than 35% of the time, the group members will be less likely to participate.

_____

ADDITIONAL INSIGHTS

8. The relationship between *faith* and *suffering* confuses many within the church of Jesus Christ. To many in the "health-wealth" or "prosperity gospel" religious movement, suffering is viewed as lack of faith, the presence of unconfessed sin, or even demon possession. What important spiritual instruction did Paul give the Philippian believers regarding faith and suffering (Philippians 1:29–30)?

_____

_____

_____

9. As you study Philippians, it's easy to become engrossed in Paul's loving relationship with this faithful church. When this happens, we may forget that the central focus of all Scripture is God rather than man. As we conclude this lesson, take a minute to review Philippians 1. What specific things did Jesus Christ do for the Philippian believers—and for you (Philippians 1:1–3, 11, 19, 29)?

_____

_____

_____

_____

_____

_____

_____

THREE

THINK LIKE JESUS

Read Philippians 2:1–11;
other references as given.

Andrew Murray, the nineteenth century South African pastor and writer, said, "Humility is not a Christian grace. It is the foundation upon which all the Christian graces exist. The fact that there is so little teaching on humility is evidence that the church doesn't see how essential humility is."

Philippians 2 presents four examples of God-centered humility: Jesus, Paul, Timothy, and Epaphroditus. No other passage in Scripture presents such a complete portrait of this essential virtue. And no Christian can truly manifest the mind of Christ without possessing genuine humility.

Now ask God to reveal Himself to you through His inspired Word and transform you into the image of Christ.

Focus Rule:

If the leader helps the group members focus on the Bible, they will gain confidence to study God's Word on their own.

———

ADD GROUP INSIGHTS BELOW

1. Many new Christians think being born again solves most of their problems in life. While salvation does answer life's greatest questions—"Can I really know God?" "What is the real meaning of life?" "Is there life after death?" "Where will I spend eternity?"—it also brings new challenges. Satan, working through sinful men (including carnal believers), causes division and disunity within the body of Christ. His goal is to turn our focus from a sinless Christ to sinful man, robbing us of joy and diminishing the church's testimony to the world.

   a. Nonbelievers are often unable to distinguish between

those who are merely religious and those who are truly born again. What new commandment did Jesus give His followers to help them live distinctly Christian lives so the unsaved could identify them as His true disciples (John 13:34–35)?

_____

_____

_____

b. What are some sins Christians commit that make it difficult for non-Christians to determine who are real believers in this world (Malachi 2:14–16; 1 Corinthians 1:11–13; 5:1–2; 6:1–5; 1 Timothy 5:13)?

_____

_____

_____

_____

2. In Philippians 2:1, Paul appealed to the Philippians to be spiritually united. Several New Testament books address the threat of spiritual division within the church (Romans 12:18; Ephesians 4:1–3; Colossians 3:12–15). Paul lists four incentives, all beginning with "if," to inspire the Philippian believers to fulfill his desire. (In the Greek, these are first-class conditional sentences, which means they are all true and can be translated, "Since there is....") What are they (Philippians 2:1)?

_____

_____

_____

_____

3. Many Christians believe God has given them the arduous task of establishing and keeping spiritual unity within the

church. Spiritual unity among God's people, however, already exists because of the work of the Holy Spirit and the bond believers have in Christ. Paul wrote these instructive words to the Ephesians: **endeavoring to keep the unity of the Spirit in the bond of peace** (Ephesians 4:3). What four things did Paul ask the Philippian believers to do to maintain spiritual unity (Philippians 2:2-4)?

1. _____
   _____ (v. ____)

2. _____
   _____ (v. ____)

3. _____
   _____ (v. ____)

4. _____
   _____ (v. ____)

Drawing Rule:

To learn how to draw everyone into the group discussion without calling on anyone, go to www.Lamplighters USA.org/training.

———

ADDITIONAL INSIGHTS

4. The common expression "Sow a thought, reap an attitude; sow an attitude, reap a lifestyle; sow a lifestyle, reap a life; sow a life, reap a destiny" is especially true when it comes to our thoughts, attitudes, and actions toward others. What specific thoughts and attitudes should every believer adopt in his relationship toward others if he wants to preserve the unity of the Spirit in the bond of peace (Philippians 2:3–4)?

    _____

    _____

    _____

5. Philippians 2 gives four examples of true humility: Christ in vv. 5–11; Paul in vv. 17–18; Timothy in vv. 19–23; and Epaphroditus in vv. 25–30. **Let this mind be in you which was also in Christ Jesus** (Philippians 2:5) is a powerful statement that is likely the theme verse of Philippians. The specific verb tense (present imperative) of the Greek word for **mind** (*phroneo*: "to think, to hold an opinion, to have

thoughts or an attitude, to be minded or disposed"; NIV 1984: "attitude") indicates a believer should be in a constant state of Christ-mindedness.

a. The Greek word for **mind** encompasses both mental understanding and the corresponding attitude that naturally results from consistent reasoning. Now that you understand the Greek word for *mind* (attitude), what do you think it means to **let this mind** (of Christ) **be in you**?

_____

_____

_____

b. The word **mind** is used frequently in Philippians (Philippians 2:2–3, 5; 3:15–16, 19; 4:2, 7). What three things must a Christian do to let the mind of Christ control his thoughts (Romans 12:1–2)?

_____

_____

_____

6. Only in Western civilization (western Europe and North America) do people think they can believe something intellectually and not act according to that belief. For example, many professing evangelicals say they're born again and believe the Bible is God's inspired Word, but they also say Jesus Christ is *not* the only way to heaven.

a. Circle the terms you *believe* are important, but your *actions* often contradict what you say you believe.

• God's Word • honesty • moral purity

• integrity • family and friends • Hell

• evangelism • prayer • forgiveness

- God's grace   - sanctity of life   - God's holiness

- sanctity of marriage   - your body as God's temple

Is your study going well? Consider starting a new group. To learn how, go to www. Lamplighters USA.org/training.

ADDITIONAL INSIGHTS

b. What must be true if what we say we believe doesn't match our actions?

_____

_____

7. Philippians 2:5–11 is the clearest passage in the Bible describing Christ's voluntary, self-sacrificing surrender. Many commentators believe these verses were part of an early Christian hymn (because of its metrical structure in the Greek). They provide a wealth of theological and ethical truth and present Christ as the ultimate example of humility.

a. The word **form** (Gk. *morphe*; NIV: "very nature") is the key to understanding Christ's true nature. There are three main interpretations for *morphe*: (1) Christ shared the same glory as the Father (John 17:5), (2) Christ shared the same perfect nature as Adam—the one Adam could have been if he had not sinned, and (3) Christ possessed the same nature as God the Father, including all the attributes and characteristics of God. Which of these three do you think best interprets the Greek word *morphe* (John 1:14, 14:6–9, 17:5; Hebrews 1:3)? Why?

_____

_____

_____

_____

_____

b. The phrase **did not consider it robbery to be equal with God** (Philippians 2:6; NIV 1984: "something to be grasped") has also been variously interpreted.

Does it mean "something that has been seized" or "something to be seized"? In other words, did Christ, in His preincarnate state, try to seize deity even though it wasn't His, or did He possess deity, but resolved not to cling to His privileged position? Which interpretation do you think is correct? Why?

_____

_____

_____

8. In Jesus Christ, we see a consistent connection between thought and the ensuing action. Because Christ didn't cling to His position with His Father, He acted consistently with His thoughts and decisions. List five distinct actions of Christ that led to man's reconciliation to God (Philippians 2:7–8).

_____

_____

_____

_____

_____

_____

_____

_____

Four

Definition of a Servant

**Read Philippians 2:12–30;
other references as given.**

In the previous lesson Jesus was presented as the ultimate example of humility. His humility led to genuine acts of sacrifice to the Father and service to man.

In this lesson we'll see that human nature, with its insatiable preoccupation with self, hasn't changed. But by the power of God, Paul, Timothy, and Epaphroditus escaped man's addictive self-centeredness and became true servants of God.

Now ask God to reveal Himself to you through His inspired Word and transform you into the image of Christ.

1. Many Bible scholars see a strong parallel between Jesus Christ's voluntary surrender (Philippians 2:5–11) and His washing of the disciples' feet during the Last Supper (John 13:4–17). In John 13:4, Jesus laid aside His outer garments; in Philippians 2:7, He laid aside His grasp on His heavenly position. In John 13:5, Jesus took a towel and wrapped it about himself (a task assigned to slaves); in Philippians 2:7, He took the form of a bondservant. In John 13:12, when Jesus finished washing the disciples' feet, He put on His outer garments and returned to the table; in Philippians 2:9, Jesus was exalted and given a name above all names. In John 13:13, Jesus acknowledged the names *Teacher* and *Lord*; in Philippians 2:11, the Bible says every tongue will confess Jesus as Lord.

Gospel Gold
Rule:

Try to get all the
answers to the
questions—not
just the easy ones.
Go for the gold.

ADD GROUP
INSIGHTS BELOW

a. What important spiritual truths do you think these two parallel passages teach about being a servant?

_____

_____

_____

_____

_____

b. What's the difference between the world's view of greatness and God's view (Mark 10:42-44)?

_____

_____

_____

c. Take a moment to think about being a servant. What one thing keeps you from a servant to God and others?

_____

_____

_____

_____

2. Jesus' death on the cross was the ultimate act of service. And He did this so we never have to perish in the lake of fire (John 3:16; Revelation 20:11–15). On the cross Jesus uttered several brief statements, including His last word, *tetelestai*, which is accurately translated **it is finished** (John 19:30). The word *tetelestai* in commercial usage referred to the satisfaction of a debt. Do you think Jesus meant (1) His earthly life was finished, (2) His ministry was done, or (3) the complete payment for man's sin was finished by His death on the cross? Why?

_____

_____

_____

Balance Rule:

To learn how to balance the group discussion, go to www.Lamplighters USA.org/training.

———

ADDITIONAL INSIGHTS

3. The excruciating pain of crucifixion is almost beyond belief. Crucifixion has been described as the world's most perfect form of torture. Jesus willingly went to the cross and endured unfathomable agony for the sins of the world—including yours.

    a. Jesus was fully God and fully man. How was the man Jesus able to bear the indescribable torture of the cross (Hebrews 12:2)?

    _____

    _____

    _____

    _____

    b. How can a believer endure the trials, persecutions, and struggles of being a true servant of God (Ephesians 6:11; Colossians 3:2, 16; Hebrews 12:2)?

    _____

    _____

    _____

    _____

    _____

4. All men will eventually kneel before Jesus Christ and confess He is the Lord (Philippians 2:10–11). Those who voluntarily surrender to Him (at salvation) before they die will be saved forever. Unfortunately, those who refuse to acknowledge Jesus as Savior and Lord will ultimately perish. Even the judgment of the eternally damned will bring glory to God because it will demonstrate His holiness (Philippians 2:11).

Knowing this coming reality of all men, how should Christians respond (2 Corinthians 5:9–11; Philippians 2:12–13)?

_____

_____

_____

_____

5. Christian author and Bible teacher Warren Wiersbe said: "Christ working for me—that's salvation. Christ working in me—that's sanctification. Christ working through me—that's service." In Scripture, man's salvation is presented as having been completed in the past on his behalf (Romans 5:1, "having been *justified*"; Romans 5:8, "Christ *died* for us"; Titus 3:5, "He *saved* us." In the Greek New Testament this point is stated even more emphatically.) The Bible, however, presents spiritual growth as an ongoing process (progressive sanctification) and a combined effort between God and the believer.

a. What do you think it means to **work out your salvation with fear and trembling** (Philippians 2:12–13)?

_____

_____

_____

b. It's God's will for every believer, including you, to become spiritually mature (Ephesians 4:14–15). What specific steps are you taking to become spiritually mature?

_____

_____

_____

_____

c. What promise(s) has God given every Christian regarding

spiritual development (Philippians 2:13)?

_____

_____

6. a. Why should every believer do all things without **complaining or disputing** (Philippians 2:14–16; NIV: "arguing")?

_____

_____

_____

   b. How can every believer do all things without complaining or arguing (1 Thessalonians 5:18; Hebrews 13:15)?

_____

_____

_____

_____

_____

_____

7. Throughout history, the church has struggled to find a biblical balance regarding its relationship to the world. Some Christians believe they should be totally separated from the world (a form of ancient monasticism also found in some modern, ultra-separatist groups). Unfortunately, isolation from the world often hinders their ability to fulfill Christ's command to make disciples (Matthew 28:18–20). On the other hand, some Christian groups become so integrated into the world's system—its values, lifestyles, philosophies— that they lose their Christian distinctiveness and witness (often called "worldliness"). How should a Christian live for God in this world without becoming isolated from the world

Has your group become a "Holy huddle?" Learn how to reach out to others by taking online leadership training.

ADDITIONAL INSIGHTS

or integrated into the world (Philippians 2:15)?

_____

_____

_____

_____

8. It's been said that some Christians are "so heavenly-minded that they are no earthly good." Many Christians, however, are so earthly-minded they are no heavenly (eternal) good. They're so immersed in this world, they've lost sight of the eternal. Like many of the pilgrims in John Bunyan's epic allegory *Pilgrim's Progress*, the glittering lights of that mythical city called Vanity Fair (the world) have enraptured them.

   a. Rather than losing sight of his eternal calling, Paul served the Lord wholeheartedly. What did he say about his willingness to serve God and the Philippians (Philippians 2:17)?

   _____

   _____

   b. Sometimes a believer's inability to assess his own culture is hindered by his lack of knowledge of other cultures, both past and present. What startling comment did Paul make about human nature that is true of every generation (Philippians 2:20–21)?

   _____

   _____

   c. How was Timothy different from the rest of the people to whom Paul referred (Philippians 2:22)?

   _____

9. Epaphroditus was a little-known but mighty servant of God.

He'd been sent by the Philippian church to deliver a financial gift to Paul and to remain in Rome to minister to his needs. Somewhere on his journey, Epaphroditus became deathly ill (Philippians 2:27, 30), and the Philippian church heard about his illness. Rather than keeping Epaphroditus with him in Rome, Paul sent him back to Philippi with the letter known as Philippians. What specific qualities did Epaphroditus possess that made him a mighty servant of God (Philippians 2:25–30)?

_____

_____

_____

_____

_____

_____

ADDITIONAL INSIGHTS

FIVE

SOLVING A SINFUL PAST

Read Philippians 3:1–8; other references as given.

The believer who possesses the mind of Christ has surrendered his will to God (chapter 1) and has become His true servant (chapter 2).

No Christian, however, can consistently serve God unless he has settled his sinful past, including his or her failures and successes. If we don't see our failures in light of God's mercy and forgiveness, Satan will embroil us in a mental maze of guilt, discouragement, and unforgiveness—robbing us of joy. A believer who doesn't see his or her successes from God's perspective will be puffed up with pride and serve self rather than God. In this study, you'll see how God enabled Paul to reconcile his sinful past, enabling him to become a mighty servant of God.

Now ask God to reveal Himself to you through His inspired Word and transform you into the image of Christ.

No-Trespassing Rule:

To keep the Bible study on track, avoid talking about political parties, church denominations, and Bible translations.

———

ADD GROUP INSIGHTS BELOW

1. **Finally,** the first word in Philippians 3:1 (Gk. *to loipon*— "furthermore; for the rest; in addition") doesn't mean Paul's letter is coming to an end, especially with 40 percent of the letter to follow. Paul instructed the Philippian church to **rejoice in the Lord** (Philippians 3:1). The command to rejoice is such a prevailing theme in Philippians that several commentators have labeled the book the "gospel of joy." Paul prayed with joy (1:4), and he rejoiced in the preaching of God's Word (Philippians 1:18). He wanted to bring the Philippians joy (1:25–26). He appealed to the Philippians to

be united for his joy (Philippians 2:1–2). He instructed the Philippians for God so he would have joy in the day of Christ (Philippians 2:16). And he encouraged the Philippians to rejoice when Epaphroditus returned to Philippi (2:28–29).

a. What do you think it means **to rejoice in the Lord** (Philippians 3:1)?

_____

_____

_____

b. Many secular counselors, including mental health professionals and health and fitness specialists, promote the benefits of a positive mental attitude in life. Some counselors even advocate prayer or meditation as part of a daily regimen for a healthy mental outlook. What do you think is the difference between having a positive mental outlook and rejoicing in the Lord?

_____

_____

_____

_____

2. It may seem strange that a prisoner (Paul) encouraged those who were free (the Philippians) to rejoice. He also reminded the Philippians that he was writing the same things he or others had previously taught publicly or had written (Philippians 3:1). Rather than apologizing for repeating himself, Paul said it was **safe** for them (Philippians 3:1, NIV 1984: "a safeguard"). List several reasons why it is a safeguard for Christians to be reminded of spiritual truth (Mark 4:15–19; Hebrews 2:1–3; 4:12; 2 Peter 2:1–2).

_____

_____

_____

_____

_____

_____

3. In Philippians 3:2, the Greek word for **beware** (*blepete*—"to be constantly on the lookout for"; NIV: "watch out") is repeated three times (**beware of dogs, beware of evil workers, beware of the mutilation**). When a word is repeated three times in the same verse, it indicates strong emphasis (Isaiah 6:3; Jeremiah 7:4; 22:29). In Philippians 3:2, **beware** emphasizes the need to be watchful for a particularly dangerous group of people.

    a. The Jews considered **dogs** the most despised and miserable of all creatures. They were homeless, vicious scavengers, usually ownerless, and lived off scraps and garbage. They regularly attacked passersby without provocation. Of whom do you think Paul was warning the Philippian believers when he said to **beware of dogs, beware of evil workers, beware of the mutilation** (2 Corinthians 11:13–22; Galatians 6:12; Philippians 3:2-6)?

        _____

        _____

        _____

    b. On another occasion Paul referred to these same false religious teachers as savage wolves (Acts 20:29–31). Why did Paul refer to them as dogs and wolves (Acts 20:29; Philippians 3:2)?

        _____

        _____

        _____

4. The apostle Peter was the first to preach to orthodox Jews in Jerusalem (Acts 2). Peter and John were the first to verify reports of the conversion of half-Jews, or Samaritans (Acts 8:14–17). Peter was even the first Christian chosen to preach to Gentiles (Acts 10; some Bible commentators see these three events as the fulfillment of Matthew 16:17–19). When the Jews learned that Peter preached to some non-Jews (Cornelius and his family), they angrily confronted Peter (Acts 11:1–3).

a. Many Jews believed that before a person could be saved, he must first become a Jew (Acts 15:1, 5). And if a Gentile became a Christian, he must do two things: accept Judaism and circumcision as proof of his willingness to become a Jew (Acts 15:5). Controversy over the Gentiles' relationship to the Law of Moses grew so intense that a church council was convened in Jerusalem (Acts 15). What four things did Peter tell the council about God's acceptance of the Gentiles and their lack of responsibility to the Law of Moses (Acts 15:8–11)?

_____

_____

_____

_____

b. What religious duties (rituals, beliefs, church traditions) *not* found in God's Word do some modern religious teachers and sects encourage their followers to accept?

_____

_____

_____

_____

_____

5. The word **circumcision** (Philippians 3:3) is used in Scripture to describe (1) physical circumcision, (2) national Israel, and (3) a person's spiritual condition before God.

    a. When the Bible uses the word **circumcision** metaphorically to describe a person's spiritual condition, what does it signify (Romans 2:28–29; Colossians 2:11)?

    _____

    b. Give three characteristics of a true worshiper of God (Philippians 3:3).

        1._____

        2._____

        3._____

6. The woman Jesus met at a well (John 4:1–42) thought worshiping God was related to a specific place (John 4:20). Like many believers today, she failed to understand that true worship is a matter of the heart—not an action limited to a particular locale. What important truth(s) did Jesus teach the woman about true worship of God (John 4:21–24)?

    _____

    _____

    _____

    _____

7. In Philippians 3:4–6, Paul sounds like he's boasting. He listed seven personal attributes: four related to his family heritage and three describing his religious devotion to Judaism. Paul's parents and his upbringing were Jewish orthodox (**circumcised the eighth day, of the stock** [NIV: "people"] **of Israel**). His family was from the tribe of Benjamin (Israel's first king, Saul, was a Benjaminite), and his native tongue was Hebrew (**a Hebrew of the Hebrews**). Paul was so zealous as a Pharisee that his personal religious conduct was blameless; he even persecuted Christians to destroy the church (Acts 9:1–2).

Use the side margins to write down spiritual insights from other people in your group. Add the person's name and the date to help you remember in the future.

———

ADDITIONAL INSIGHTS

a. Being merely religious may make you morally fit, but it cannot fit you for heaven. How did Paul assess his pedigreed Jewish heritage and his impeccable religious devotion before salvation (Philippians 3:7–8)?

_____

_____

b. Paul used the word **rubbish** (Gk. *skubalon*—"human excrement, food rejected by the body as non-nutritious, refuse or leavings of a feast, or food thrown away from the table") to describe the eternal benefits of his religious efforts before salvation (Philippians 3:8). Why do you think Paul considered his family heritage and past religious devotion as **loss** and **rubbish**?

_____

_____

_____

8. In Philippians 3:7–8, Paul used the word **count** (Gk. *egeomai* — "to consider [NIV], reckon, or count") three times. The repeated use of this word emphasizes Paul's diligence when he compared the value of his religious self-effort to the riches and value of Christ. In verse 7, Paul used a past tense of the word (**counted,** NIV: "now consider" [Greek perfect tense]), but in verse 8 he changed to the present tense of the verb (**count**). What important spiritual truths are taught by the use of this specific word, its repeated use, and the conspicuous change from the past (counted) to the present tense (count)?

_____

_____

_____

_____

_____

Six

KNOWING CHRIST

Read Philippians 3:9–21; other references as given.

The Bible is God's inspired revelation to man. The apostle Paul wrote these words to Timothy (and us): **All Scripture is inspired by God and is profitable for doctrine** (how to live right), **for reproof** (where we went wrong), **for correction** (how to get back on the right path), **for instruction in righteousness** (how to stay on the right path) (2 Timothy 3:16, paraphrased).

In the previous lesson God showed Paul where he went wrong. In this lesson, we'll see how Paul got on the right path in life and what he needed to do to stay there.

Now ask God to reveal Himself to you through His inspired Word and transform you into the image of Christ.

Transformation Rule:

Seek for personal transformation, not mere information, from God's Word.

———

ADD GROUP INSIGHTS BELOW

1. In many of his New Testament letters, Paul spoke confidently about his relationship with Christ and his eternal destiny (Philippians 1:23; 2 Timothy 1:12). In Philippians 3:8–9, however, Paul's statement **that I may gain Christ and be found in Him** could imply uncertainty about his salvation and eternal destiny. If Paul was confident about his relationship to Christ, what do you think he meant by this statement?

   _____

   _____

   _____

   _____

2. Many Jews believed a person must keep the Old Testament Law of Moses to be saved (Acts 15:1). Today, many Jews and Gentiles still believe they must keep some moral or religious code to gain eternal life. What do the following verses teach about man's good works and their eternal merit before God?

a. Isaiah 64:6: _____

_____

b. Romans 3:20: _____

_____

c. James 2:10: _____

_____

3. Millions of religious, churchgoing people believe they can earn God's acceptance and gain eternal life by doing good works. Tragically, at the final judgment, they will proclaim their loyalty to Christ only to hear Jesus' sobering words of eternal rejection, **Depart from Me** (Matthew 7:21–23). How can a person have complete assurance he will be accepted by God into eternal life (Philippians 3:9)?

_____

_____

_____

4. When a person trusts Jesus Christ alone for salvation, God gives him eternal life, and he will never perish (John 10:28–29; 19:30). While salvation is the end of man's need for eternal acceptance from God, it's also the beginning of a whole new life (2 Corinthians 5:17). The Bible says, **through whom** [Jesus] **also we have obtained our introduction by faith into this grace** (Romans 5:2). What do you think is meant by the following statements?

a. **that I may know Him** (Philippians 3:10) _____

_____

_____

b. **that I may know … the power of the resurrection** (Philippians 3:10)_____

_____

_____

c. **that I may know … the fellowship of His sufferings, being conformed to His death** (Philippians 3:10)

_____

_____

_____

5. Paul's statement **I may attain to the resurrection from the dead** (Philippians 3:11) is perhaps the most difficult verse to interpret in the book of Philippians. What do you think Paul meant by this statement?

_____

_____

_____

6. A person's past can be either an emotional labyrinth— extremely tortuous and complex—or a ladder on which the individual can reach higher in life. When Paul assessed his religious efforts before conversion, his good works were worthless (loss, rubbish) before God. What additional truths did God reveal to Paul to help him overcome his sinful past, including his aggressive persecution of the church (1 Timothy 1:12–14)?

_____

_____

_____

It's time to choose your next study. Turn to the back of the study guide for a list of available studies or go online for the latest studies.

_____

ADDITIONAL
INSIGHTS

_____

_____

7. Many modern counselors, including some Christian counselors, believe counselees must revisit their past before they can live victoriously for Christ. Paul, however, overcame his troubled past by acknowledging his sin, evaluating his pre-salvation life from God's perspective, embracing God's forgiveness, and pressing forward for Christ.

   a. Do you think a Christian should focus on the past, on God's character, or on both, to overcome his struggles? Please explain your answer.

   _____

   _____

   _____

   _____

   b. Jesus conducted one of the shortest counseling sessions in history when an adulterous woman was brought to Him (John 8:3–11). Jesus' actions and words reveal at least three principles that every Christian can use to counsel someone living in sin. Please list them (John 8:3–11).

   _____

   _____

   _____

   _____

   _____

8. Paul wanted the Philippians to know that he had not reached spiritual perfection (Philippians 3:12: **not that I have already attained [it] or am already perfected**), even though his

goal was to know Christ and become all God wanted him to be. Some Christians are so passive in their Christian lives they never reach spiritual maturity. Some mistakenly think it is God's job to make them spiritually mature, and others are just lazy or self-centered.

a. What words or phrases does Paul use to describe his longing to know Christ (Philippians 3:12–14)?

_____

_____

_____

_____

b. What words would you (and those closest to you) use to describe your spiritual appetite or motivation?

_____

_____

_____

_____

9. In the Greek New Testament, the verb tense of **forgetting** (Philippians 3:13, Greek — *epilanthanomai*) indicates Paul was in the continuous action of forgetting the past (**those things which are behind**).

a. What important truth(s) do you think Paul's statement teaches regarding his past failures?

_____

_____

_____

b. What should every Christian do to fulfill God's will for his life (Philippians 3:13–14; Hebrews 12:1–3)?

_____

Would you like to learn how to prepare a life-changing Bible study using a simple 4-step process? Contact Lamplighters and ask about ST-A-R-T.

———

ADDITIONAL INSIGHTS

47

_____

_____

_____

_____

10. It is God's will for every believer to know Christ deeply and every church to live in unity (Ephesians 4:1–6, 11–16). To fulfill God's will, all Christians must let the mind of Christ dominate their thinking (Philippians 3:16, **let us be of the same mind**). Unfortunately some people within the church are not so minded. How does Paul describe those whose minds and desires are focused on earthly things rather than on God (Philippians 3:18–19)?

_____

11. The Bible uses three powerful word pictures to help Christians understand their relationship to God and to other believers: (1) Believers are various parts of a body, with Jesus as the head (1 Corinthians 12:12–27; Ephesians 4:15–16). This picture emphasizes the believer's need to respond to Christ and the Christian's interdependence on other Christians. (2) Believers are building stones in a house under construction (Ephesians 2:20–22; 1 Peter 2:5–8), with Christ as the chief cornerstone and the apostles and prophets as the foundation. This illustration emphasizes the church's solid foundation and the ongoing building of the church. (3) Describe the third word picture, and explain the important spiritual truth(s) taught by this illustration (Philippians 3:20–21; 2 Corinthians 5:20; Ephesians 6:19–20).

_____

_____

_____

_____

_____

SEVEN

PEACE OF MIND

Read Philippians 4:1–7;
other references as given.

Having the mind of Christ is not optional for believers; it is the essence of being a true follower of Jesus Christ. When believers allow thoughts to control them rather than controlling their thoughts through the power of God, they've been deceived, believing their thoughts are uncontrollable, external entities.

In this lesson Paul instructs every believer to take control of his thoughts, proving that God gives every believer the power to control his or her thinking. Is it easy to exercise mental discipline? Absolutely not! But it is essential to fulfill God's will for your life and experience the peace and joy He promises every believer.

Now ask God to reveal Himself to you through His inspired Word and transform you into the image of Christ.

Many groups study the Final Exam the week after the final lesson for three reasons: (1) someone might come to Christ, (2) believers gain assurance of salvation, (3) group members learn how to share the gospel.

ADD GROUP
INSIGHTS BELOW

1. In Philippians 4:1, Paul powerfully expressed his deep love for the Philippians and reminded them to **stand fast** (NIV: "stand firm") in the Lord. The Greek word for **stand fast** (*steko*—"to stand, to stand firm, to hold one's ground") also describes the determination needed by a soldier not to move, even one inch, from his assigned position.

    a. What must a Christian do to stand fast in the Lord as God commanded (1 Corinthians 16:13; Galatians 5:1–3; Ephesians 6:10–18; Philippians 1:27)?

_____

49

_____

_____

_____

_____

b. In 1 Corinthians 16:13, four bold statements (including **stand fast in the faith**) remind believers to be good soldiers for Jesus Christ. When Christians think of being faithful to Christ, they often use phrases like "having faith in God," "trusting Christ," "relying on God's Word," and "walking in the Spirit." They seldom use the phrase **be brave** (NIV: "be courageous"). What do you think it means to be a brave follower of Christ, and in what area(s) of your life can you be more courageous for the Lord?

_____

_____

_____

2. Paul referred to the Philippians as his **joy and crown** (Philippians 4:1). The Greek word *stephanos* was used to describe the crown of a conqueror, the laurel of victory, or a festive garland. A different Greek word, *diadema*, was used to describe a king's crown. Many Christians never realize they can win eternal crowns for faithful service for God. List four crowns available to all believers; the one reserved for faithful, God-called pastors; and the spiritual conduct necessary to win each (1 Corinthians 9:24–27; 1 Thessalonians 2:19–20; 2 Timothy 4:5–8; James 1:12; 1 Peter 5:2–4).

_____

_____

_____

_____

_____

_____

_____

If the leader asks all the study questions, the group discussion will be more likely to stay on track.

ADDITIONAL INSIGHTS

3. Standing fast or firm in the Lord includes working with other believers for the cause of Christ and the salvation of the lost (Philippians 1:27). Unfortunately, Satan deceives some Christians into causing strife and contention between God's people, which diminishes the church's witness for Christ to the world (John 13:34–35).

   a. In Philippians 4:2–3, Paul addressed two women whose interpersonal problem threatened the unity and the witness of the Philippian church. Paul's counsel to the women and the church reveals several important principles that can help believers when they counsel others. Please name at least four.

   1. _____

   2. _____

   3. _____

   4. _____

   b. Paul asked an unnamed third person (Philippians 4:3, **true companion**; NIV 1984 — "loyal yokefellow") to assist the two women in the reconciliation process. When should a third party become involved in a conflict between believers (Philippians 4:3; Matthew 18:15–18; 1 Corinthians 6:1–8; Galatians 6:1)?

   _____

   _____

   _____

   _____

   _____

4. Paul said Clement and the fellow workers' names were written in the **Book of Life** (Philippians 4:3). What does the Bible teach about this important book (Revelation 3:5; 13:8; 20:11–15; 21:22–27)?

    _____

    _____

    _____

    _____

5. Paul counseled both the church and the women before returning to one of the dominant themes of the book— joy in the Lord. This time he adds emphasis by repeating the command to **rejoice** and adding the word **always** (Philippians 4:4). The Greek construction (present active imperative) of the command to rejoice means Christians should never cease rejoicing. Rather than complaining or arguing (Philippians 2:14), believers should joyfully praise God for working *all* things together for good (Romans 8:28).

    a. Take a minute to examine your life before God. In what area(s) of your life can you express trust in God by being more joyful?

        _____

        _____

        _____

    b. What do complaining and being frustrated with life reveal about a believer's walk with God?

        _____

        _____

    c. Unfortunately, some Christians consider the commands to **do all things without complaining and disputing** (Philippians 2:14) and to **rejoice in the Lord always** (Philippians 4:4) as suggestions rather than direct commands from God. What does the Bible teach about disobeying God's commands, even those that seem optional or hard to obey (James 4:17)?

_____

_____

If you realize you're more a complainer than one who regularly rejoices in the Lord, what can you do to change?

_____

_____

_____

It's time to order your next study. Allow enough time to get the books so you can distribute them at the Open House. Consider ordering 2-3 extra books for newcomers.

———

ADDITIONAL INSIGHTS

6. Instead of complaining and arguing, believers should praise God and rejoice in the Lord. What other godly quality should be present in every believer's life (Philippians 4:5)? What should motivate believers to manifest this important character quality in their lives (Philippians 4:5)?

    _____

    _____

    _____

7. The relationship between rejoicing and being gentle (Philippians 4:5) and prayer should not be overlooked. Instead of complaining to men, a Christian should take his burdens to God in prayer. Instead of being harsh with others, he should ask God for a gentle spirit. Instead of being fearful and anxious, he should pray with supplication and thanksgiving, trusting God for the outcome.

    a. What do you think is the difference between prayer and supplication (Philippians 4:6)?

        _____

        _____

        _____

b. Believers are to let their **requests be made known to
God** (Philippians 4:6). Some Christians, however, are
reluctant to ask God for specific prayer requests because
they feel they're bothering God, or they're afraid He
won't answer their prayers. What do the following verses
teach about prayer (Hebrews 4:16; James 4:1–3; 1 Peter
3:7)?

_____

_____

_____

_____

8. Christian theologian Millard Erickson said the ultimate
expression of worldliness in a believer's life is a prayerless
life. Author Daniel Henderson said a believer's unwillingness
to pray is his declaration of independence from God. The
unsaved cannot pray, and the proud will not pray.

a. What promise is given to the believer who learns how to
pray to God in faith (Philippians 4:7)?

_____

_____

b. According to one survey, only 8 percent of the things
people worry about actually occur. Take a minute to
examine your life. What things are you tempted to worry
about rather than praying and leaving the results to
God?

_____

_____

_____

_____

EIGHT

TAKING THOUGHTS CAPTIVE

Read Philippians 4:8–23; other references as given.

God wants every believer to **have this mind in you which was also in Christ Jesus** (Philippians 2:5). To do this, you must have a surrendered mind, a servant mind, a settled mind, and a sanctified mind.

In this final lesson Paul thanks the Philippians for their generous financial gift, calling it a sweet-smelling aroma and sacrifice to God. When a believer has the mind of Christ, he'll also have a heart for others.

Now ask God to reveal Himself to you through His inspired Word and transform you into the image of Christ.

1. Paul began the final section of his letter by instructing the Philippians to limit their thinking to certain things (Philippians 4:8). The particular form of the Greek word for **meditate** (*logidzomai*—"to consider, to reckon, to take into account, to think on"; NIV: "think about") is a command that should continue without stopping. This command has profound implications for all Christians, especially those who regard their thoughts, feelings, and emotions as external, random entities that are only partially controllable. God's command to think or meditate on certain things implies that God has given believers the ability to control their thoughts.

    a. List the eight areas believers are commanded to think about (Philippians 4:8).

Final Exam:

Are you meeting next week to study the Final Exam? To learn how to present it effectively, contact Lamplighters.

———

ADD GROUP INSIGHTS BELOW

1. _____

2. _____

3. _____

4. _____

5. _____

6. _____

7. _____

8. _____

b. Take a minute to examine the words, ideas, and thoughts that enter your mind through printed material (books, magazines), electronic media (television, Internet, music), and interpersonal communication. Do your thoughts meet the eight qualifications for biblical thinking (Philippians 4:8)?

_____

If not, what decisions do you think God wants you to make—decisions that will free your mind and give you peace, freedom, and more joy in the Lord?

_____

_____

_____

_____

2. Many Christians don't believe God wants to set them free from paralyzing thoughts of fear, anxiety, doubt, anger, lust, unforgiveness, and bitterness. Some Christians rationalize their sinful thoughts—"I've always been fearful" or "Our family has always had a problem with anger." Others turn to a variety of prescription or nonprescription ways of medicating pain instead of letting God take their burdens and heal their hearts.

a. Why should a believer surrender every sinful, human thought to God and accept His perspective on all matters of life (Isaiah 55:6–9)?

_____

_____

b. How can a Christian control his thoughts so they're pleasing to God and result in peace and joy (Proverbs 3:5–7; John 8:31–32; 2 Corinthians 10:4–5)?

_____

_____

_____

_____

_____

_____

Would you like to learn how to lead someone through this same study? It's not hard. Go to www.Lamplighters USA.org to register for *free* online leadership training.

———

ADDITIONAL INSIGHTS

3. In Philippians 4:9 (paraphrasing), the apostle says, "Whatever I taught you, whatever you received, whatever you heard me say, and whatever you saw me do, do it— follow my example." Some may consider Paul's statement prideful. But Paul's confidence was based on his knowledge of and confidence in God and His Word. What do you think is the difference between learning and receiving God's truth (Philippians 4:9)?

_____

_____

_____

_____

_____

4. The prophet Moses led over two million Israelites out of Egypt. Moses faithfully taught God's Word to the people, but most of them perished in the wilderness. Many Christians live

in a spiritual wilderness of doubt, unbelief, and confusion. In the book of Hebrews, the writer compares the plight of the ancient Israelites to New Testament believers.

a. What important warning did the writer of Hebrews give Christians regarding *learning* and *receiving* the truth (Hebrews 2:1–3)?

_____

_____

b. Every week millions of Christians attend worship services where God's Word is faithfully preached, but their lives show little evidence of genuine change. Why doesn't faithfully preaching and teaching God's Word affect their lives (Hebrews 4:1–2)?

_____

_____

_____

5. Paul thanked the Philippians for their financial gift sent by way of Epaphroditus (Philippians 4:10–19). Paul said the Philippians' care had **flourished again** (Gk. *anathallo*—"to shoot up, to blossom again, to put forth new shoots"; NIV: "renewed"), indicating they had expressed love in tangible ways in the past (Philippians 4:10). What did Paul say about his personal financial situation at the time he wrote this letter (Philippians 4:11–12)?

_____

_____

_____

_____

6. Paul said he learned how to be full (NIV: "to have plenty") and to suffer need, indicating he understood how to live for the Lord in riches and in poverty (Philippians 4:12). What must a believer understand before he can be content in

every financial circumstance (Job 1:13–21; Psalm 24:1; James 1:9–11)?

_____

_____

_____

_____

_____

_____

_____

7. The phrase **I can do all things through Christ who strengthens me** (Philippians 4:13) is often a Christianized version of the world's erroneous statement, "You can be anything you want to be." Look carefully at the immediate context in which this verse is located (Philippians 4:10–19). Please give a more precise definition or meaning of Paul's statement?

_____

_____

_____

8. Paul remembered the financial assistance given him by the Philippians when he was at Thessalonica (Philippians 4:16).

    a. How did Paul describe the ultimate end of the financial gifts he received from the Philippians (Philippians 4:17)? Why do you think he used the term "fruit" (NRSV: "profit")?

    _____

    _____

    b. Many Christians never consider financial stewardship, including giving to the work of the Lord, as an act of worship. What words or phrases did Paul use to help

Did you know Lamplighters is more than a small group ministry? It is a discipleship training ministry that uses a small group format to train disciple-makers. If every group trained one person per study, God would use these new disciple-makers to reach more people for Christ.

———

ADDITIONAL
INSIGHTS

59

the Philippians understand their financial gift was a genuine act of worship (Philippians 4:18)?

_____

_____

_____

c. How can you make your financial offerings to the Lord more of an act of worship?

_____

_____

_____

9. Philippians 4:19 is often claimed by Christians as an unconditional promise from God. Based upon the preceding passage, what must believers do before they can claim this significant promise (Philippians 4:17– 18)?

_____

_____

10. You have come to the end of this challenging study on the book of Philippians.

a. What are the most significant spiritual truths you've *learned* from studying Philippians?

_____

_____

_____

b. What are the most significant spiritual truths you've *received* from studying Philippians?

_____

_____

_____

LEADER'S GUIDE

Lesson 1: Seeing God's Hand in Change

1. a. 1. Lydia, a merchant from Thyatira, and her family (Acts 16:14–15).
      2. A slave girl (Acts 16:16–18). Nothing indicates whether she was saved.
      3. A jailor and his family (Acts 16:27–34).
   b. Paul and Silas told the jailor he had to "Believe on the Lord Jesus Christ" (Acts 16:31).

2. The entire Philippian church (all the saints). The bishops or overseers. The deacons.

3. 1. A deacon must be respectable as an individual and respected by others (1 Timothy 3:8, reverent).
   2. A deacon must be a man of verbal integrity (1 Timothy 3:8, **not double-tongued**). He should not be two-faced. The Greek phrase could refer to not being a gossip or talebearer. A deacon is likely aware of personal information about those in the church, so he must be discreet with this information.
   3. A deacon must not be a heavy drinker or a drunkard (1 Timothy 3:8, **not given to much wine**).
   4. A deacon must not cheat others in financial matters or be materialistic (1 Timothy 3:8).
   5. A deacon must be mature in the faith. He must hold the deep truths of the faith and maintain a pure conscience (1 Timothy 3:9).
   6. A deacon must demonstrate a life of virtue and integrity before being allowed to serve in the office of deacon (1 Timothy 3:10, **let these also first be tested; then let them serve as deacons**).
   7. A deacon must have a godly wife and family (1 Timothy 3:11–12).

4. A normal Christian person. Paul used the word *saint* in 1 Corinthians 1:2 to describe the Corinthian believers who were *not* living godly lives. In the New Testament, saint refers to a believer's legal standing before God.

5. 1. Paul was thankful for their partnership in the work of the Lord.

2. Paul was thankful for their spiritual faithfulness over the years (from the first day until now).

6. a. God, who began the work of redemption in them at their salvation, will continue to work in them through the process of sanctification. God will continue this work until He is finished and they receive their reward from Jesus Christ.

   b. Christians must diligently pursue spiritual maturity. Once we are saved, we must pursue virtue (right conduct in thought and action), knowledge (an understanding of God that goes beyond salvation to a working knowledge of His nature and His will), self-control (willingness to forsake the appetites of the flesh and come under the Holy Spirit's control), perseverance (a growing ability to endure the hardships of life for the glory of God and the advancement of the gospel), godliness (daily manifesting the life of Christ), brotherly kindness (gentleness in thought, word, and action that reflects Christ's character); and love (a consistent rejection of self-centered living and the adoption of the sacrificial heart of Christ that seeks God's eternal best for all mankind).

   c. 1. The believer will never be barren (2 Peter 1:8).
      2. The believer will never be unfruitful (2 Peter 1:8).
      3. The believer will experience assurance of his salvation (2 Peter 1:9–10).
      4. The believer will never stumble in his Christian life (2 Peter 1:10).
      5. The believer will receive a rich welcome into God's eternal kingdom (2 Peter 1:11).

7. a. The judge will be Jesus Christ himself, and the place of judgment is known as the judgment seat of Christ.

   b. The believer's motives and thoughts, as well as his actions and deeds.

   c. Answers will vary.

8. *Defending* the gospel is the critical ministry of responding to the lies and false accusations of ungodly men and women who attack the claims of Christ and the authenticity and authority of God's Word. The lies are often presented as doubts about the plain meaning of Scripture and the authority of God's Word. *Confirming* the gospel is the positive presentation of God's message so that listeners are convinced of biblical truth by seeing the interrelatedness of Scripture.

9. a. Paul prayed that their love (for God and man) would increase. The more the Philippians understoodGod's love, the more they could love others in a godly way and make the wisest choices in life (approve the things that are excellent).

   b. Paul's ultimate goal for the Philippians was for them to be sincere (holy and pure), good witnesses (without offense), and filled with Christ's righteousness in their daily living.

Lesson 2: The Purpose of Life

1. a. 1. The gospel was advanced (Philippians 1:12).
      2. The palace guard learned that Paul's imprisonment was because of faith in Christ (Philippians 1:13).
      3. Most of the Christians became bold witnesses for Christ (Philippians 1:13).

   b. 1. God often reveals His plans to His servants through a change in circumstances.
      2. God may direct His servants toward a new place of ministry that may not be obvious at first.
      3. When God redirects His servants, He may reveal His plan only later.

2. He rejoiced that the gospel was being preached. He also said, "I will rejoice," indicating he determined to rejoice in the future if the same situation occurred.

3. a. Paul was pleased for the gospel to be preached. Since he had no control over the motives and actions of those preaching the Word, he chose to rejoice that the Word was preached.

   b. Paul's statement demonstrates the need for the gospel to be preached to the lost. It's important for God's people to serve Him with pure motives, but the desperate condition of the lost (under the wrath of God and without hope, Ephesians 2:1, 12) and the power of the gospel should compel believers to preach the message of Christ's redemption with a sense of divine urgency.

   c. Answers will vary.

4. a. I will glorify and exalt Christ during my life and at my death. I will not bring shame on Christ's name by my actions, and I will boldly witness for my Savior. I will live for Christ because He is the essence of my life, and my eternal reward will be greater than anything I experience here on earth.

   b. Answers will vary.

5. a. Heaven. Answers will vary.

   b. An ambassador for Christ who works to reconcile the world to God.

   c. During their time on earth, these saints patiently waited to dwell in a heavenly city whose builder and maker is God (Hebrews 11:10). They died believing in God's promises, even though they never realized them on earth. They were certain God's promises would eventually be fulfilled (assured, embraced them, Hebrews 11:13). They were strangers and pilgrims on earth (Hebrews 11:13). The way they lived indicated they were seeking another homeland (Hebrews 11:14). Even though they could have returned to their former lives, they sought a better, heavenly country. As a result, God was unashamed to be called their father, and He prepared a city for them (Hebrews 11:16).

6. These two truths should transform every Christian into a vital witness for Christ. Since heaven is the believer's real home, he should live for Christ wholeheartedly as an ambassador. His life should be so committed to Christ that others see him living for God and waiting patiently for his eternal reward. He shouldn't be concerned if his wants aren't met here on earth, because the best is yet to come.

7. 1. They were to live for God and work together for the advancement of the gospel by being united in mind and spirit (Philippians 1:27).

   2. They were not to be terrified by their adversaries (Philippians 1:28).

   3. They were to realize that God called some of them to salvation *and* suffering (Philippians 1:29).

8. God has given many people the faith to believe in Christ for salvation. God has also given some believers the privilege of suffering for Christ.

9. 1. He changed sinners into saints (Philippians 1:1).

   2. He gave us grace and peace (Philippians 1:2).

   3. He accepted us into God's family (Philippians 1:3).

4. He gave us the fruits of righteousness (Philippians 1:11).
5. He answers our prayers and gave us the help of the Holy Spirit (Philippians 1:19).
6. He gave us salvation and the privilege of suffering for His Name (Philippians 1:29).

Lesson 3: Think like Jesus

1. a. Believers are commanded to love other Christians in the same way Christ loves us.
   b. Divorce (Mal. 2:14–16). Factions, favoritism, and cliques (1 Corinthians 1:11–13). Immorality (1 Corinthians 5:1, 2). Lawsuits against other Christians (1 Corinthians 6:1–5). Unforgiveness (2 Corinthians 2:6–8). Gossip about other people and meddling in other people's lives (1 Timothy 5:13).

2. 1. If (since) there is real encouragement in life because you belong to Christ.
   2. If (since) there is genuine comfort from knowing the love of Christ.
   3. If (since) you experience close fellowship (with God) as a result of the Holy Spirit's presence in your life.
   4. If (since) you have any affection and mercy.

3. 1. They were to be like-minded, which means they were to live for God's glory and the advancement of the gospel.
   2. They were to have the same love for Christ and each other. No one was to lag behind in loving God and others.
   3. They were to be united in spirit (one accord). They were to work together for God's glory without violating God's unique design and gifting of each individual.
   4. They were all to think and act consistent with the mind of Christ and the will of God.
   5. A believer should do nothing motivated by selfishness or pride. He should be humble in heart and action, and he should value others as more important than himself (Philippians 2:3). In addition to his own needs, he should look out for the interests and needs of others (Philippians 2:4).

4. A believer must aggressively reject self-centered living and pride (Philippians 2:3). To accomplish this, he must consistently value others more than himself (Philippians 2:3). He must also demonstrate genuine humility and be more concerned with other's needs than his own (Philippians 2:4).

5. a. A Christian must allow Jesus Christ to be Lord over all aspects of life, the Holy Spirit to be his counselor and guide into all truth, and the Word of God to be the final authority for every decision.

   b. 1. A believer must present his life as a living sacrifice to God.

      2. A believer must reject the values (goals, priorities, etc.) of this world.

      3. A believer must constantly allow his mind to be renewed by the Word of God.

6. a. Answers will vary.

   b. We must not really believe what we think and say we believe.

7. a. The third interpretation. Christ possesses the same nature as the Father, including all the attributes, characteristics, and glory (John 1:14; 14:6–9; 17:5; Hebrews 1:3).

   b. Jesus Christ resolved not to cling to His position in heaven and the glory He possessed before His incarnation. Several Bible scholars believe He surrendered the voluntary use of His divine attributes during His earthly ministry.

8. 1. Christ willingly surrendered His exalted position in heaven.

   2. Christ accepted the role of a servant.

   3. Christ came to earth in the likeness or form of a man.

   4. Christ humbled himself even after He became a man.

   5. Christ went to the cross to die for man.

Lesson 4: Definition of a Servant

1. a. 1. To be a servant, an individual must yield his grip or hold on any existing earthly position.

      2. To be a servant, an individual must willingly embrace the position of a servant.

3. To be a servant, an individual must be willing to serve others in humble ways.

b. The world views greatness by how many people serve those in authority. In the world system, the greatest men have the most servants. Jesus said the greatest men would be the servants of all.

c. Answers will vary.

2. The complete payment for man's sin was finished. The Greek word (*tetestai*) was used in the ancient world to indicate that a debt had been paid in full.

3. a. Jesus looked past the agony of the cross to the joy He would experience for all eternity, knowing His sacrifice paid the penalty for man's sin.

b. 1. A believer must put on the whole armor of God (Ephesians 6:11).

2. A believer must fix his attention on eternity (Colossians 3:2).

3. A believer must let the Word dwell richly in his life and learn to apply God's wisdom. He needs to meditate on God's Word (Colossians 3:16). He also needs to talk about truth with other believers; they must encourage each other with psalms, hymns, and spiritual songs.

4. A believer must keep his eyes on Jesus Christ (Hebrews 12:2).

4. 1. Christians should live in a way that pleases the Lord (2 Corinthians 5:9).

2. Christians should do everything they can to reach others for Christ (2 Corinthians 5:11).

3. Christians should take their Christian life seriously and seek to grow in Christ. They should realize God will give them the desire to be all they can be for Christ and the grace to accomplish His will (Philippians 2:12–13).

5. a. God gives Christians the responsibility to participate in their own spiritual progress. Salvation is a gift from God, but spiritual growth depends upon our willingness to submit to God's Word and to walk by the Spirit. Believers should diligently work with God to become spiritually mature.

b. Answers will vary.

c. God gives believers both the desire and the grace to become spiritually mature.

6. a. Christians should do all things without complaining or disputing (arguing) so they are above reproach (**blameless, harmless**) as believers and good witnesses (**shine as lights**) for God to a lost world (**crooked and perverse generation**).
    b. 1. A Christian must learn to trust God and praise Him for whatever He allows to come into his life. A believer must understand the doctrine of sovereignty and that what God brings into his life is His will, whether blessings or trials (1 Thessalonians 5:18).
        2. Christians must learn to give a sacrifice of praise to God for whatever He allows to enter our lives (Hebrews 13:15). A sacrifice is often something costly and difficult to give. In the same way God's people must learn to offer the sacrifice of praise for all things God allows. When we do this, we demonstrate faith in God in spite of our earthly circumstances.

7. The Bible advocates neither spiritual isolationism (monasticism) nor spiritual immersion (worldliness). Believers are to live distinctly Christian lives in the midst of an ungodly society. To do this, a believer must be blameless in his conduct and harmless in his dealings with others. If he lives a godly life, he will shine as a beacon of light in a world corrupted by the darkness of sin.

8. a. Paul said he would be glad and rejoice if his entire life was spent helping them become all God wanted them to be.
    b. People are all naturally self-centered and uninterested in serving Jesus Christ.
    c. Like Paul, Timothy served the Lord faithfully.

9. Epaphroditus—a Christian **brother**, a servant of God (**fellow worker**), and a true disciple of Jesus Christ (**fellow soldier**)—was sent by the Philippian church to serve Paul (Philippians 2:25). Knowing the church heard he almost died (Philippians 2:26), Epaphroditus had a deep passion and concern for them. He was a man to be held in high esteem (Philippians 2:29) and was so faithful to God that he risked his life to serve Paul and the Philippian church (Philippians 2:30).

Lesson 5: Solving a Sinful Past

1. a. A believer constantly rejoices in the person of Christ and revels in what Christ has done on his behalf. A believer also trusts in God's sovereign plan over all aspects of life, expressing this trust in private and public gratitude and praise to God and man.

   b. A positive mental attitude is man-centered and incapable of comprehending God and His plan for man. Although a positive mental attitude provides some benefits to an unsaved person, it often leads to self-deception and denial of the realities of life and the condition of man's soul (lost, depraved). When an individual rejoices in the Lord, his faith and confidence are in God, not in his mind and its ability to process life.

2. 1. Satan tries to steal the seed of God's Word sown in a believer's heart (Mark 4:15).

   2. Trials and difficulties often cause Christians to temporarily struggle in their relationship with God (Mark 4:17).

   3. Daily concerns of life and the innate human desire to accumulate wealth can preoccupy believers with other things, choking the Word out of their lives (Mark 4:19).

   4. Christians are tempted to neglect their salvation. When this happens, they drift away from the truth (Hebrews 2:1–3).

   5. God's Word is alive and has the ability to examine a believer's actions and motives (Hebrews 4:12).

   6. There are false religious teachers who deceive people. Hearing truth helps protect believers from being led into theological error (2 Peter 2:1–2).

3. a. They were Jewish false teachers who taught that all followers of Jehovah must observe the Law of Moses.

   b. They reminded Paul of a pack of wild dogs or savage wolves because they followed him around, attempting to undermine his missionary work. As scavengers, they attacked infant churches and new believers after Paul left to continue his missionary work.

4. a. 1. God gave the Holy Spirit to both Jews and Gentiles (Acts 15:8).

      2. God made no distinction between Jews and Gentiles, saving (purifying) both groups by faith (Acts 15:9).

      3. Jews shouldn't obligate Gentiles to keep the Law of Moses that the Jews themselves couldn't keep (Acts 15:9).

      4. Salvation for Jews and Gentiles is through the grace of the Lord Jesus Christ (Acts 15:11).

  b. Answers will vary widely.

5. a. Individual salvation.

    b. 1. He worships God in the Holy Spirit.

        2. He rejoices in Jesus Christ.

        3. He places no confidence in his flesh.

6. 1. True worship is related to a person (God) rather than a place (John 4:21–22). Believers should worship God at all times, not just on Sundays.

    2. True worshipers of God worship Him in Spirit and truth (John 4:23).

    3. God seeks those who worship Him in spirit and truth (John 4:23).

    4. Because God is Spirit, those who worship Him must worship in spirit and truth. Interestingly, this prerequisite is not presented as a suggestion or recommendation. It's an imperative (must worship) that becomes a qualification for the only type of worship God accepts.

7. a. Loss (Philippians 3:7). Rubbish (Philippians 3:8).

    b. Paul counted his former religious devotion as loss and rubbish because it did not give him eternal life, and God rejected it.

8. In Philippians 3:7, Paul referred in the past tense (counted) to a time in his past (likely at salvation) when he concluded (through the Holy Spirit's conviction) that his personal religious devotion was worthless. After Paul's conversion, while writing Philippians, he continued to evaluate the inferior worth of everything other than Christ. This continuous counting all things as loss likely contributed to Paul's great desire to follow Christ. Unfortunately, some Christians never bother to compare the perishable values of temporal things to the riches of Christ.

Lesson 6: Knowing Christ

1. Paul wasn't satisfied to just be saved. Since Jesus gave His all for man, Paul wanted to give his all for Christ. He wanted to know everything he

could about Christ—he wanted to gain Christ. To be found in Him (Christ) means the same thing. Whether at death or at Christ's return to earth, Paul wanted to be found in perfect union and fellowship with Christ.

2. a. Isaiah 64:6—All of man's righteousness (his attempts to gain favor with God apart from Christ) are like filthy rags to God.
   b. Romans 3:20—No man's deeds (good works) are good enough to justify him before God.
   c. James 2:10—It takes only one sin (**stumble in one point**) to be declared guilty before God.

3. An individual must place his faith in Christ alone (**the righteousness which is from God by faith**) for salvation and have no confidence in his own efforts (**my own righteousness**) to gain eternal life.

4. a. Paul longed to know Christ even more intimately and personally than as Savior.
   b. Paul wanted to experience in his personal life the power that raised Christ from the grave. Paul realized he'd been raised with Christ (Colossians 3:1), and he knew this same resurrection power was available to help him live victoriously for Christ.
   c. Paul wanted to know Christ's deepest comfort in his trials, tribulations, and inner struggles. Every faithful follower of Jesus Christ knows an earthly loneliness as a pilgrim and stranger in a world hostile to Christ and His disciples. Only Christ can comfort and encourage believers because He also suffered (**fellowship of His sufferings**). Paul wanted Christ's consolation, and he could experience it only if he was dead to self and alive to Christ (**conformed to [Christ's] death**).

5. Paul, in humility and modest confidence, hoped his life and ministry would receive God's blessed endorsement and he would experience the resurrection of the redeemed during his lifetime.

6. 1. Paul's *actions* were not only sinful, *he* was sinful (blasphemer, a persecutor, an insolent man (1 Timothy 1:13). Man needs to understand that he not only sins but also that he is a sinner. His problem is not with acts of sin but his sinful nature. Only when he comprehends his sinful nature can he understand his need for a Savior. Until then, he remains

deceived and tries to sin less.

2. It was God who did not count (same Greek word as in Philippians 3:7–8) or hold Paul's past sins against him (1 Timothy 1:12).

3. Paul didn't choose the gospel ministry. Jesus Christ chose Paul, a man with a sinful past, to serve Him.

4. God's forgiveness enabled Paul to understand that his past was past (1 Timothy 1:13, **I was formerly**).

5. God gave Paul mercy and exceedingly abundant grace (1 Timothy 1:12–13).

6. When Paul sinned greatly, he acted ignorantly because of not knowing God (1 Timothy 1:13, **unbelief**).

7. a. A Christian should foous on Jesus Christ. In some cases, it may be necessary to explore the past to deal with unresolved guilt due to unconfessed sin, exposing false guilt and lies. However, Paul's willingness to acknowledge his sin, and his knowledge of God's character (including His mercy and grace), set him free of the past. Paul dealt with his past from God's perspective, sought and accepted His complete forgiveness, and moved forward without looking back.

   b. 1. Jesus eliminated the accusers so He could talk directly with the woman (John 8:7–9).

   2. Jesus told the woman He didn't condemn her—He was there to help her (John 8:10).

   3. Jesus informed the woman that her problem was sin (John 8:11), not an addiction, sickness, or any other inescapable condition.

   4. Jesus focused on the real issue, not the symptom (John 8:11).

   5. Jesus told her she could stop immediately (John 8:11, **Go and sin no more**). By this statement, Jesus gave her hope that she could change immediately and her life could be transformed. She could escape the cycle of sin. When counselors redefine sin, calling it by nonbiblical terms, they often think they're being merciful. On the contrary, they are stripping the counselee of the hope of Christ's deliverance and forgiveness.

8. a. **I press on** (Philippians 3:12). **That I may lay hold** (Philippians 3:12). **Reaching forward** (Philippians 3:13). **I press toward the goal for the prize** (Philippians 3:14).

   b. Answers will vary.

9. a. Paul was in a constant state of forgetting his past. Satan is the accuser of the brethren (Revelation12:10), and every time Satan tempted Paul by reminding him of past failures, Paul deliberately dismissed the accusation. Paul acknowledged he acted ignorantly in unbelief, accepted God's mercy and grace, walked in freedom, and served the Lord.

    b. Walk in humility (**I do not count myself to have apprehended**, Philippians 3:13); deal with the past and then forget it (**forgetting those things which are behind**, Philippians 3:13); accept responsibility to be all God wants you to be (**press forward toward the goal**, Philippians 3:14); lay aside all sin and the things that hinder your spiritual progress (Hebrews 12:1); keep your focus entirely on Jesus Christ (Hebrews 12:2); and don't let yourself grow weary or discouraged (Hebrews 12:3).

10. Enemies of the cross of Christ (Philippians 3:18).

11. Believers are citizens of heaven (Philippians 3:20) who serve Jesus Christ as His ambassadors on earth (2 Corinthians 5:20; Ephesians 6:20). Our goal is to be good ambassadors for Jesus Christ and to reconcile the world to God (2 Corinthians 5:20).

Lesson 7: Peace of Mind

1. a. 1. A believer must be alert to spiritual danger and be courageous in faith (1 Corinthians 16:13).
        2. A believer must not allow himself to become entangled in legalism (Galatians 5:1–3). To do this, a Christian must understand law and grace (the believer's relationship to the Old Testament Law of Moses and New Testament grace) and who he is in Christ.
        3. A believer must put on the whole armor of God (Ephesians 6:10–16).
        4. A believer must walk in the Spirit and be united with other members of the body of Christ (Philippians 1:27).

    b. To be a brave follower of Jesus Christ means to obey God's Word consistently (not just in the presence of God's people), honor Christ in every area of your life, and live for Him without compromise. Answers will vary.

2. 1. The *imperishable* crown (1 Corinthians 9:24–27). This crown will be awarded to believers who live wholeheartedly for Christ and live disciplined Christian lives.
   2. The crown of *rejoicing* (1 Thessalonians 2:19–20). This crown will be awarded to believers who lead others to salvation in Christ.
   3. The crown of *righteousness* (2 Timothy 4:5–8). The crown will be awarded to believers who love the doctrine of Christ's return.
   4. The crown of *life* (James 1:12). This crown will be awarded to believers who find strength to overcome temptation and trials in life through the power and love of God.
   5. The crown of *glory* (1 Peter 5:2–4). This crown will be awarded to obedient pastors who faithfully preach God's Word.

3. a. 1. Paul didn't take sides.
      2. Paul addressed the problem openly. Since the problem was public knowledge, he addressed it publicly. This way, the entire church and the two women knew what was expected. Paul didn't want the problem to continue, eventually causing disunity.
      3. Paul attacked the problem rather than the people causing the problem.
      4. Paul reminded the church of each woman's past faithfulness to the Lord.
      5. Paul instilled hope by giving positive counsel.
      6. Paul encouraged an unnamed third party to help resolve the problem.
   b. 1. A third party should get involved when people can't resolve the problem by themselves or it becomes public knowledge (Philippians 4:3).
      2. A third party should get involved when he's asked to witness a meeting between disputing believers and sin is involved (Matthew 18:15–18).
      3. A third party should get involved when one believer is considering taking another Christian to court (1 Corinthians 6:1–8).
      4. A third party should get involved only after examining his own heart, adopting a genuine spirit of humility, and committing to restore an erring brother in a spirit of love (Galatians 6:1).

4. 1. Names of people can be blotted out of the Book of Life (Revelation 3:5).

2. Only those names that haven't been blotted out of the Book of Life will worship God. The Book of Life is also called the **Book of Life of the Lamb** (Jesus Christ, Revelation 13:8).

3. The evil works of those who are eternally lost are recorded in the Book of Life, and they are judged accordingly (Revelation 20:11–15). None of the people who will be judged at the Great White Throne judgment (Revelation 20:11) will be saved. The judgment will determine the degree of punishment they will receive for all eternity (Revelation 20:13–15).

4. Only those whose names are still written in the Book of Life (the redeemed) will enter the new Jerusalem (the city, Revelation 21:23) and its temple (Revelation 21:22).

5. a. Answers will vary.
   b. He doesn't understand God, the doctrine of sovereignty, his relationship to God, and his responsibility as a child of God.
   c. It is sin. Answers will vary.

6. Gentleness. The Greek word (*epieikes*) suggests a forbearing, gracious, nonretaliatory spirit. The nearness of God.

7. a. The Greek word for *prayer* (*proseuche*) is a general term describing a believer's approach to God. The word for *supplication* (Gk. *deesei*) is used to emphasize specific requests one makes to God for himself and others.
   b. 1. Believers can come boldly to God and receive mercy and grace in their times of need (Hebrews 4:16).
      2. God wants His people to ask Him so He can answer their prayers (James 4:2).
      3. Some prayers are not answered because they are self-centered and not according to God's will (James 4:1–3).
      4. Husbands need to live with their wives in an understanding way so their prayers are unhindered (1 Peter 3:7).

8. a. The believer will receive God's peace, which will guard and protect his mind and thoughts.
   b. Answers will vary.

Lesson 8: Taking Thoughts Captive

1. a. True. Noble. Just. Pure. Lovely. Good report. Virtue. Praiseworthy.
   b. Answers will vary. Answers will vary.

2. a. God's ways are higher than man's ways, and His thoughts are higher than man's thoughts.
   b. 1. A believer must trust in the Lord with all his heart and not lean on his own understanding (Proverbs 3:5).
      2. A believer must acknowledge God by responding to His Word in every aspect of life (Proverbs 3:6).
      3. A believer must humble himself before God and depart from evil (Proverbs 3:7).
      4. A believer must deliberately try to understand and obey God's Word (John 8:32).
      5. A believer must discipline his mind and bring every thought captive to Jesus Christ (2 Corinthians 10:4–5).

3. *Learning* refers to a student's progressive intellectual understanding of a truth or concept. *Receiving* refers to a student's personal acceptance of a truth or concept. Learning involves mental comprehension of a truth, and receiving involves heartfelt adoption and ownership of the truth.

4. a. God's people shouldn't neglect their salvation. If they neglect their salvation by not obeying His Word, they will drift away from the Lord (Hebrews 2:1–3).
   b. Some worshipers are satisfied to simply hear God's Word preached, so they don't apply it to their lives (Hebrews 4:1–2).

5. Paul had learned to be content in whatever financial circumstance God gave him, even if he was hungry and suffering need (Philippians 4:11).

6. 1. God is the one who gives and takes away (Job 1:13–21). At any moment, God can give or take away what He has entrusted to an individual.
   2. Everything and everyone belong to God (Psalm 24:1).
   3. Both rich and poor can glorify God in their financial situation. The poor man can rejoice knowing God has given him the riches of Christ (**his exaltation**, James 1:9). The rich man can rejoice knowing God has

revealed to him the transitory nature of life (James 1:10); this helps him remember that life doesn't consist of the things he owns.

7. In the immediate context the verse means a believer can learn to glorify God in whatever condition (including times of great financial need or in abundance) he finds himself in. As a general principle, it likely means that God's people can glorify Him in all circumstances. The verse does not mean Christians can do anything they set their hearts to, disregarding God's sovereign plan for their lives.

8. a. Fruit. Paul saw the Philippians' gift from an eternal perspective, and their financial gift, used by Paul to reach lost souls for Christ, became spiritual fruit that God credited to their eternal account.
   b. A sweet-smelling aroma. An acceptable sacrifice. Well-pleasing to God.
   c. Answers will vary.

9. Believers must support the work of the Lord before they can claim this great promise.

10. Answers will vary.

FINAL EXAM

Every person will eventually stand before God in judgment—the final exam. The Bible says, **And it is appointed for men to die once, but after this the judgment** (Hebrews 9:27).

May I ask you a question? *If you died today, do you know for certain you would go to heaven?* I did not ask if you're religious or a church member, nor did I ask if you've had some encounter with God—a meaningful spiritual experience. I didn't even ask if you believe in God or angels or if you're trying to live a good life. The question I *am* asking is this: *If you died today, do you know for certain you would go to heaven?*

When you die, you will stand alone before God in judgment. You'll either be saved for all eternity, or you will be separated from God for all eternity in what the Bible calls the lake of fire (Romans 14:12; Revelation 20:11–15). Tragically, many religious people who believe in God are not going to be accepted by Him when they die.

> **Many will say to Me in that day, "Lord, Lord, have we not prophesied in Your name, cast out demons in Your name, and done many wonders in Your name?" And then I will declare to them, "I never knew you; depart from Me, you who practice lawlessness!"** (Matthew 7:22–23)

God loves you and wants you to go to heaven (John 3:16; 2 Peter 3:9). If you are not sure where you'll spend eternity, you are not prepared to meet God. God wants you to know for certain that you will go to heaven.

> **Behold, now is the accepted time; behold, now is the day of salvation.** (2 Corinthians 6:2)

The words **behold** and **now** are repeated because God wants you to know that you can be saved today. You do not need to hear those terrible words, **Depart from Me ....** Isn't that great news?

Jesus himself said, **You must be born again** (John 3:7). These aren't the words of a pastor, a church, or a particular denomination. They're the words of Jesus Christ himself. You *must* be born again (saved from eternal damnation) before you die; otherwise, it will be too late when you die! You can know for certain today that God will accept you into heaven when you die.

These things I have written to you who believe in the name of the Son of God, that you may* know *that you have eternal life.

(1 John 5:13)

The phrase ***you may know*** means that you can know for certain before you die that you will go to heaven. To be born again, you must understand and accept four essential spiritual truths. These truths are right from the Bible, so you know you can trust them—they are not man-made religious traditions. Now, let's consider these four essential spiritual truths.

Essential Spiritual Truth

#1

The Bible teaches that you are a sinner and separated from God.

No one is righteous in God's eyes. To be righteous means to be totally without sin, not even a single act.

There is none righteous, no, not one;
There is none who understands;
There is none who seeks after God.
They have all turned aside;
They have together become unprofitable;
There is none who does good, no, not one.
(Romans 3:10–12)

...for all have sinned and fall short of the glory of God.
(Romans 3:23)

Look at the words God uses to show that all men are sinners—**none**, **not one**, **all turned aside**, **not one**. God is making a point: all of us are sinners. No one is good (perfectly without sin) in His sight. The reason is sin.

Have you ever lied, lusted, hated someone, stolen anything, or taken God's name in vain, even once? These are all sins.

Are you willing to admit to God that you are a sinner? If so, then tell Him right now you have sinned. You can say the words in your heart or aloud—it doesn't matter which—but be honest with God. Now check the box if you have just admitted you are a sinner.

☐ God, I admit I am a sinner in Your eyes.

Now, let's look at the second essential spiritual truth.

Essential Spiritual Truth

#2

The Bible teaches that you cannot save yourself or earn your way to heaven.

Man's sin is a very serious problem in the eyes of God. Your sin separates you from God, both now and for all eternity—unless you are born again.

For the wages of sin is death.
(Romans 6:23)

And you He made alive, who were dead in trespasses and sins.
(Ephesians 2:1)

Wages are a payment a person earns by what he or she has done. Your sin has earned you the wages of death, which means separation from God. If you die never having been born again, you will be separated from God after death.

You cannot save yourself or purchase your entrance into heaven. The Bible says that man is **not redeemed with corruptible things, like silver or gold** (1 Peter 1:18). If you owned all the money in the world, you still could not buy your entrance into heaven. Neither can you buy your way into heaven with good works.

> *For by grace you have been saved through faith, and that not of yourselves; it is the gift of God, not of works, lest anyone should boast.* (Ephesians 2:8–9)

The Bible says salvation is **not of yourselves**. It is **not of works, lest anyone should boast**. Salvation from eternal judgment cannot be earned by doing good works; it is a gift of God. There is nothing you can do to purchase your way into heaven because you are already unrighteous in God's eyes.

If you understand you cannot save yourself, then tell God right now that you are a sinner, separated from Him, and you cannot save yourself. Check the box below if you have just done that.

☐ God, I admit that I am separated from You because of my sin. I realize that I cannot save myself.

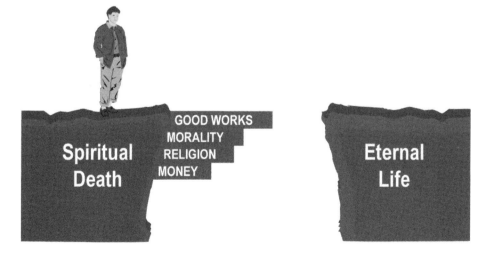

Now, let's look at the third essential spiritual truth.

Essential Spiritual Truth

#3

The Bible teaches that Jesus Christ died on the cross to pay the complete penalty for your sin and to purchase a place in heaven for you.

Jesus Christ, the sinless Son of God, lived a perfect life, died on the cross, and rose from the dead to pay the penalty for your sin and purchase a place in heaven for you. He died on the cross on your behalf, in your place, as your substitute, so you do not have to go to hell. Jesus Christ is the only acceptable substitute for your sin.

> *For He [God, the Father] made Him [Jesus] who knew [committed] no sin to be sin for us, that we might become the righteousness of God in Him.*
> (2 Corinthians 5:21)

> *I [Jesus] am the way, the truth, and the life. No one comes to the Father except through Me.*
> (John 14:6)

Nor is there salvation in any other, for there is no other name under heaven given among men by which we must be saved.
(Acts 4:12)

Jesus Christ is your only hope and means of salvation. Because you are a sinner, you cannot pay for your sins, but Jesus paid the penalty for your sins by dying on the cross in your place. Friend, there is salvation in no one else—not angels, not some religious leader, not even your religious good works. No religious act such as baptism, confirmation, or joining a church can save you. There is no other way, no other name that can save you. Only Jesus Christ can save you. You must be saved by accepting Jesus Christ's substitutionary sacrifice for your sins, or you will be lost forever.

Do you see clearly that Jesus Christ is the only way to God in heaven? If you understand this truth, tell God that you understand, and check the box below.

❐ God, I understand that Jesus Christ died to pay the penalty for my sin. I understand that His death on the cross was the only acceptable sacrifice for my sin.

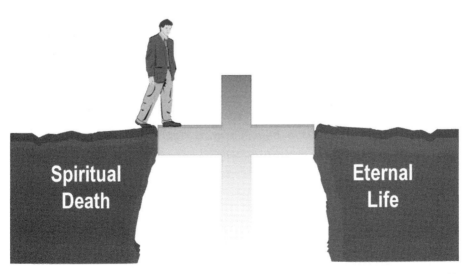

Spiritual Death

Eternal Life

Essential Spiritual Truth

#4

By faith, you must trust in Jesus Christ alone for eternal life and call upon Him to be your Savior and Lord.

Many religious people admit they have sinned. They believe Jesus Christ died for the sins of the world, but they are not saved. Why? Thousands of moral, religious people have never completely placed their faith in Jesus Christ *alone* for eternal life. They think they must believe in Jesus Christ as a real person and do good works to earn their way to heaven. They are not trusting Jesus Christ *alone*. To be saved, you must trust in Jesus Christ *alone* for eternal life. Look what the Bible teaches about trusting Jesus Christ alone for salvation.

Believe on the Lord Jesus Christ, and you will be saved.
(Acts 16:31)

...that if you confess with your mouth the Lord Jesus and believe in your heart that God has raised Him from the dead, you will be saved. For with the heart one believes unto righteousness, and with the mouth confession is made unto salvation.... For there is no distinction between Jew and Greek, for the same Lord over all is rich to all who call upon Him. For "whoever calls on the name of the Lord shall be saved.
(Romans 10:9–10, 12–13)

Do you see what God is saying? To be saved or born again, you must trust Jesus Christ *alone* for eternal life. Jesus Christ paid for your complete salvation. Jesus said, **It is finished!** (John 19:30). Jesus paid for your salvation completely when He shed His blood on the cross for your sin.

If you believe that God resurrected Jesus Christ (proving God's acceptance of Jesus as a worthy sacrifice for man's sin) and you are willing to confess Jesus Christ as your Savior and Lord (master of your life), you will be saved.

Friend, right now God is offering you the greatest gift in the world. God wants to give you the *gift* of eternal life, the *gift* of His complete forgiveness for all your sins, and the *gift* of His unconditional acceptance into heaven when you die. Will you accept His free gift now, right where you are?

Are you unsure how to receive the gift of eternal life? Let me help you. Do you remember that I said you needed to understand and accept four essential spiritual truths? First, you admitted you are a sinner. Second, you admitted you were separated from God because of your sin and you could not save yourself. Third, you realized that Jesus Christ is the only way to heaven—no other name can save you.

Now, you must trust that Jesus Christ died once and for all to save your lost soul. Just take God at His word—He will not lie to you! This is the kind of simple faith you need to be saved. If you would like to be saved right now, right where you are, offer this prayer of simple faith to God. Remember, the words must come from your heart.

God, I am a sinner and deserve to go to hell. Thank You, Jesus, for dying on the cross for me and for purchasing a place in heaven for me. I believe You are the Son of God and You are able to save me right now. Please forgive me for my sin and take me to heaven when I die. I invite You into my life as Savior and Lord, and I trust You alone for eternal life. Thank You for giving me the gift of eternal life. Amen.

If, in the best way you know how, you trusted Jesus Christ alone to save you, then God just saved you. He said in His Holy Word, ***But as many as received Him, to them He gave the right to become the children of God*** (John 1:12). It's that simple. God just gave you the gift of eternal life by faith. You have just been born again, according to the Bible.

You will not come into eternal judgment, and you will not perish in the lake of fire—you are saved forever! Read this verse carefully and let it sink into your heart.

Most assuredly, I say to you, he who hears My word and believes in Him who sent Me has everlasting life, and shall not come into judgment, but has passed from death into life.
(John 5:24)

Now, let me ask you a few more questions.

According to God's holy Word (John 5:24), not your feelings, what kind of life did God just give you? _____

What two words did God say at the beginning of the verse to assure you that He is not lying to you? _____ _____

Are you going to come into eternal judgment? ☐ YES ☐ NO

Have you passed from spiritual death into life? ☐ YES ☐ NO

Friend, you've just been born again. You just became a child of God.

To help you grow in your new Christian life, we would like to send you some Bible study materials. To receive these helpful materials free of charge, e-mail your request to **info@LamplightersUSA.org.**

Spiritual Death

Eternal Life

Appendix

Level 1 (Basic Training)
Student Workbook

To begin, familiarize yourself with the Lamplighters' *Leadership Training and Development Process* (see graphic on page 90). Notice there are two circles: a smaller, inner circle and a larger, outer circle. The inner circle shows the sequence of weekly meetings beginning with an Open House, followed by an 8–14 week study, and concluding with a clear presentation of the gospel (Final Exam). The outer circle shows the sequence of the Intentional Discipleship training process (Leading Studies, Training Leaders, Multiplying Groups). As participants are transformed by God's Word, they're invited into a discipleship training process that equips them in every aspect of the intentional disciple-making ministry.

The Level 1 training (Basic Training) is *free*, and the training focuses on two key aspects of the training: 1) how to prepare a life-changing Bible study (ST-A-R-T) and 2) how to lead a life-changing Bible study (10 commandments). The training takes approximately 60 minutes to complete, and you complete it as an individual or collectively as a small group (preferred method) by inserting an extra week between the Final Exam and the Open House.

To begin your training, go to www.LamplightersUSA.org to register yourself or your group. A Lamplighters' Certified Trainer will guide you through the entire Level 1 training process. After you have completed the training, you can review as many times as you like.

When you have completed the Level 1 training, please consider completing the Level 2 (Advanced) training. Level 2 training will equip you to reach more people for Christ by learning how to train new leaders and by showing you how to multiply groups. You can register for additional training at www. LamplightersUSA.org.

Intentional Discipleship
Training & Development Process

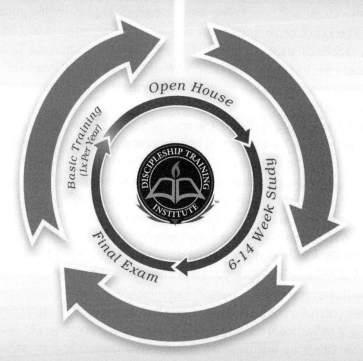

Multiplying Groups

The 5 Steps of Faith for Starting Studies
Training Library
Online Resources

Leading Studies

ST-A-R-T
10 Commandments
Solving All Group Problems

Open House

Basic Training (1x Per Year)

6-14 Week Study

Final Exam

Training Leaders

4 Responsibilities of a Trainer   *4 Levels of Student Development*
Leadership Training   *3 Diagnostic Questions*

John A. Stewart © 2017

How to Prepare a Life-Changing Bible Study

ST-A-R-T

Step 1: _____ and _____.

Pray specifically for the group members and yourself as you study God's Word. Ask God (_____) to give each group member a rich time of personal Bible study, and thank (_____) God for giving you a desire to invest in the spiritual advancement of each other.

Step 2: _____ the _____.

Answer the questions in the weekly lessons without looking at the

_____ _____.

Step 3: _____ _____and _____.

Review the Leader's Guide, and _____ every truth you missed when you originally did your lesson. Record the answers you missed with a _____ _____ so you'll know what you missed.

Step 4: _____ _____.

Calculate the specific amount of time _____ _____ to spend on each question and write the start time next to each one in the _____ using a _____.

How to Lead a Life-Changing Bible Study

10 COMMANDMENTS

1	2	3
4	5	6
7	8	9
	10	

Lamplighters' 10 Commandments are proven small group leadership principles that have been used successfully to train hundreds of believers to lead life-changing, intentional discipleship Bible studies.

Essential Principles for Leading Intentional Discipleship Bible Studies

1. The 1st Commandment: The _____ Rule.
   The Leader-Trainer should be in the room _____ minutes before the class begins.

2. The 2nd Commandment: The _____-_____ Rule.
   Train the group that it is okay to _____, but they should never be _____.

3. The 3rd Commandment: The _____ Rule.
   _____, _____, _____ ask for _____ to _____ the _____, _____, and _____ the questions. The Leader-Trainer, however, should always _____ the questions to control the _____ of the study.

4. The 4th Commandment: The ____:____ Rule.
   _____ the Bible study on time and _____ the study on time _____ _____. No exceptions!

5. The 5th Commandment: The _____ Rule.
   Train the group participants to _____ on God's Word for answers to life's questions.

1	2	3
4 **59:59**	5	6
7	8	9
	10	

6. The 6th Commandment: The _____ Rule.
   Deliberately and progressively _____ _____ participants into the
   group discussion over a period of time.

7. The 7th Commandment: The _____ _____ Rule.
   _____ the participants to get _____ the answers to the
   questions, not just _____ or _____ ones.

8. The 8th Commandment: The _____ Rule.
   _____ the group discussion so you _____ the
   lesson _____ _____ and give each question _____
   _____.

9. The 9th Commandment: The _____-_____ Rule.
   Don't let the group members talk about _____
   _____, _____ _____, or
   _____ _____.

10. The 10th Commandment: The _____ Rule.
    _____ God to change lives, including _____.

1 _____	2 _____	3 _____
4 **59:59** _____	5 _____	6 _____
7 _____	8 _____	9 _____
	10 _____	

Choose your next study from any of the following titles

- John 1-11
- John 12-21
- Acts 1-12
- Acts 13-28
- Romans 1-8
- Romans 9-16
- Galatians
- Ephesians
- Philippians

- Colossians
- 1 & 2 Thessalonians
- 1 Timothy
- 2 Timothy
- Titus/Philemon
- Hebrews
- James
- 1 Peter
- 2 Peter/Jude

Additional Bible studies and sample lessons
are available online.

For audio introductions on all Bible studies,
visit us online at www.Lamplightersusa.org.

Looking to begin a new group?
The Lamplighters Starter Kit includes:

- 8 James Bible Study Guides
  (students purchase their own books)
- 25 Welcome Booklets
- 25 Table Tents
- 25 Bible Book Locator Bookmarks
- 50 Final Exam Tracts
- 50 Invitation Cards

For a current listing of live and online discipleship training
events, or to register for discipleship training, go to
www.LamplightersUSA.org/training.

Become a Certified
Disciple-Maker or Trainer

Training Courses Available:

- Leader-Trainer
- Discipleship Coach
- Discipleship Director
- Certified Trainer (Level 1)

Contact the Discipleship Training Institute
for more information (800-507-9516).

The Discipleship Training Institute is a ministry of
Lamplighters International.